SUFISM

Ross Books
Berkeley, Calif.

ISBN 0-89496-038-5

Ross Books
P.O. Box 4340
Berkeley, Calif.
94704

TABLE OF CONTENTS

Foreword 5
   Islamic Sects 6
   Names 6
   Summary 8

Key Dates, Words, People & Works In Sufism 11

THE THEORY, PRACTICES AND ORIGINS OF SUFISM

Chapter 1: General Background 17
   History 17
   The Morshed 19
   The Salek 20
   Ablution 21
   The Khaneghah 22
   The Khergheh 23

Chapter 2: Sufi Theory and Terminology 27
   Literature and practice 27
   The Forty Stages 34

Chapter 3: Influences and Origins 43
   Sufism and Sophism 43
   The "Wearers of Wool" 45
   Safa 45
   Tasawof 46
   The Origins of Sufism 48
   Sufism and Buddhism 49
   The First Sufis 51

THE CENTERS OF SUFISM: PAST AND PRESENT

Chapter 4: Historical Centers of Baghdad,
Khurasan and Shiraz 55
The Center at Baghdad 55
The Center at Khurasan 58
The Center at Shiraz 63

Chapter 5: The Present Centers of Kurdestan,
Karaj and the Remaining Branches of Sufism in Iran 67
Center at Kurdestan 67
Center at Karaj 72
The Remaining Branches 78

Chapter 6: The Oveyssi School of Sufism at Karaj . . 85
The Master of the School 92
Sessions of the School 93
Ceremonies Where the Cloak is Worn 96
Seyr Va Solook 97

Appendix (Footnotes to chapters) 99

References 105
Glossary 108
Index 111

FOREWORD

Throughout the centuries there has been a great deal of confusion as to what the Sufi faith is all about. How did it start? What are their practices? Where are the major orthodox Sufi centers of today and what are their lineages?

In an effort to clarify these points, the author decided to visit the homeland of the Sufi people, translate some of the more important documents and bring back with him a significant contribution to our understanding of the Sufi life. Persia (now Iran) is where the major concentration of traditional Sufi culture has existed over recent history and consequently a trip to Iran was made. Due to the recent strife in that area of the world, it is all the more important that works of this religious culture are translated and preserved.

In the next sections of the forward, I will provide information on Islamic sects and Sufi names as they designate religious affiliations before turning to the more detailed material which forms the body of this work. Readers totally unfamiliar with the world of Islam would otherwise be confused when reading the text.

Islamic Sects

The Islamic faith has two major sects, the Sunni and the Shiite. There are a number of smaller sects but they do not compare with the estimated 15 million Shiite and 145 million Sunni. The Sunni and Shiite differ primarily in that the Shiite sect feels that upon the death of the prophet Mohammad, the son in law of Mohammad (Imam Ali) was the next leader of the Islamic faith. The Sunni, on the other hand, ascribe equal importance to three other contemporary religious leaders. The Shiite sect therefore has some special ceremonies that commemorate the death of Imam Ali that the Sunni do not.

Although the exact status of Imam Ali is the source of many bitter arguments between the Sunni and Shiite sects, both sects do respect Imam Ali as one of the great religious figures and when you hear Islamic people of either sect call on Ali or pray to Ali, it is usually to Imam Ali that they speak.

Names

In addition to being a Sunni or Shiite, one may also be Darvish or Sufi. The word Darvish and the word Sufi are the same. Sufism originated with **Mohammad**, as will be shown in this book, and the first followers of Sufism migrated to India as well as to the Arab countries. With almost no communication with other followers and no formal name for their religion, the Indian followers became known as "Darvish". The Persian followers, in the meantime, became known as "Sufi". They are the same religion, however, as both have the same original lineage.

The names used to describe the religious affiliations of people may seem confusing until you understand what you are looking for. Once you understand, however, things are quite clear. For example, in addition to being Sufi, a given person will have a particular teacher and place of worship. Thus, you may have a Shiite Sufi from the Oveyssi school of Sufism at the city of Karaj.

To further clarify things: Suppose almost all of the people that go to the Oveyssi school are Shiite. We can then say that all followers of the Oveyssi lineage are Sufis and all these Sufis are Shiite and all Shiites are Islamic but not vice-versa.

We can say that this naming process is very common in almost all religions. In Christianity, for example, you have the Catholic faith as one of the dominant sects. There also exists a monastic Catholic order called the Carmelites (founded in the 12th century on Mt. Carmel in Syria). The Carmelites have monasteries all over the world. Each monastery has a name. In Kingston, California, for example, the monastery is called "The Carmelite Order of Christ the Exhiled King". We can therefore say that there exist some people that are Christian Catholic Carmelites from The Carmelite Order of Christ the Exhiled King at Kingston. The name looks confusing at first but it is not when you understand what you are looking for. It is also clear that all Carmelites are Catholic and all Catholics are Christian but not vice-versa.

While we are using a Christian analogy, there is one other thing we should mention about Sufi names. For the sake of illustration, let's suppose you are a Christian Carmelite nun. Also, suppose you were taught at the Mt. Carmel monestary in Syria. Furthermore, suppose that over the centuries there have been two really outstanding Sisters that have taught at the Mt. Carmel monestary and every great student of the Carmelite order has probably at least heard of them in the literature. Let's call them Sister Smith and Sister Brown. Now, if you are in the company of other people that are very familiar with Carmelite literature and teachings, you can let people quickly understand what you believe in if you say that you are a Carmelite nun from Mt. Carmel and a follower of the lineage of Sister Smith and Sister Brown. Everyone will immediately know a great deal about your belief. This is exactly what the Sufis do. For example, in the geographic region of Iran known as Kurdestan there is a group of Sunni Sufis that are called the Ghaderi-ie. They named their order after Abd al-Ghader (circa 1166 A.D.). There are some people that will incorporate the name of the school or lineage in their personal name.

Therefore, if you are reading religious literature or meeting religious people you will frequently encounter a very long name for a person. If it is not a family lineage they are giving you, the reason for the long name is probably that they are incorporating in their name the names of the masters or schools that they follow so that you will get the location of their school and the lineage of their teachings in one name. This is important if you are reading literature because it helps you classify or understand a given person's place in history.

Summary

In summary, then, Sufism is a cultural-religious system, based on Islam, for a significant section of the populations of Turkey, Iraq, South Africa and Iran. Since Persia has, throughout history, been the main location for the orthodox Sufi faith, I will trace in this work the history of Sufism in Iran from its origins to the present day. The first part of the book will provide the reader with an explanation of the main principles, theories and practices of Sufism; the second part will trace in detail the development of the different centers of Sufism in Iran. We will look at the historical (no longer extant) centers of Baghdad, Khurasan and Shiraz, to the present-day centers of Kurdestan and Karaj. For the convenience of the reader, a chart containing various key words, dates and names in Sufism has been provided on the following pages. A glossary is included in the back and should be referred to whenever necessary. Notes to each chapter will be found in the appendices, along with a bibliography.

It is my intention that this book should be accessible to a wide range of people from differing backgrounds. For this reason, I have presented detailed historical lineages along with a broader explanation of the theories and practices of Sufism today, with the hope that both the novice and the scholar studying the subject may gain some profit and insight from my research.

Dr. Ronald Grisell
Berkeley, Calif.
Fall, 1982

KEY DATES, WORDS, PEOPLE, AND WORKS IN SUFISM

Key Dates:	Christian	Islamic
Birth of Mohammad	571 A.D.	50 B.H *
Mohammad's vision that he should go out into the world as a prophet.	612 A.D.	10 B.H.
Mohammad's move from Mecca to Medina. (Marks the beginning of the Islamic calendar.)	622 A.D.	1 A.H.
Death of Mohammad	635 A.D.	13 A.H.
Imam Ali and the other caliphs collect together the teachings of Mohammad, as revealed to him through God, and turn them into a written book, the Koran.	645 A.D.	23 A.H.

*B.H.: Before Hejrat; A.H.: After Hejrat.

Key Words:

Caliph: Among Islamics, a judge, governor, or one in power, in either civil or religious capacity. (Also written: Calif, Kalif, khalif, khaliff.)

Imam: Islamic title meaning "Guide".

Khaneghah: Sufi place of worship, similar in appearance to a mosque.

Khergheh or Robe: The woolen cloak passed on from Mohammad to a succession of Sufi Masters.

Morshed: A master (in the sense of "instructor") of Sufism.

Salek: A follower of Sufism.

Sheikh: An experienced man in Sufism.

Tasawof: To become a "Sufi" (means "purity").

Key People:

Imam Ali: Mohammad's cousin and son in law; first Master of the Shiite sect. There are two major sects of Sufism (and of Islam): the Shiite and the Sunni. Their main difference of opinion is in their respective attitudes to the preeminence of Imam Ali. The former believe that he is the only chosen master of Sufism. The Sunni, on the other hand, ascribe equal importance to three other contemporary caliphs.

Mohammad: Founding Prophet of the religion.

Oveys Gharani: A follower of Mohammad, the Prophet, who succeeded his Robe. Died 37 A.H.

Salman Farsi: The Persian and one of the first eight followers of
Mohammad.

Key Works:

"Forty Stages": Work by Seyed Ali Hamedani, expanding Attar's
seven stages into forty.

Ghoshariri's Treatise: Treatise which sets out code of Sufi behavior.

The Koran: The Holy Book of Islam.

"Seven Stages of the Heart": Work by Sheikh Farid-al-din Attar, in
which the seven main steps towards achieving gnosis are
explained.

The Theory, Practices

and Origins of

Sufism

Chapter 1

General Background

History

To cultivate an understanding of Sufism, a look at its historical origins is useful. In Iran and in neighboring countries, Sufism is closely related to Islam. Its origins find root with the advent of the Prophet Mohammad in the 6th century A.D.

Mohammad was born in Mecca, Saudi Arabia, circa 572 A.D. His father, who died two months before his birth, was a poor man but belonged to the Koreish, one of the distinguished Arabian tribes. While yet a young man, Mohammad married a wealthy widow and was thereby relieved of the necessity of daily labor and given leisure to indulge in religious contemplation. At that time, although Judaism and Christianity had been adopted by certain Arabian tribes, idolatrous worship had supplanted most of their ancient rites. Mohammad would annually go to Mt. Hira to meditate and pray. One year, upon returning from the mountain, Mohammad declared himself a chosen prophet of God. He preached in Mecca for 9 years and gained a number of adherants. As one might expect, this caused friction with other established beliefs. Finally, in 612 A.D., he was warned by his followers that his enemies intended to murder him and he was forced to flee

Mecca to **Medina**. This flight marks the beginning of the Islamic calendar and is called 1 A.H. ("*After Hejrat*" meaning "after the flight or migration"). Mohammad had a number of followers both in Mecca and in the surrounding country. His flight allowed him to gather his followers and, in 630 A.D., he returned to wrest Mecca from the hands of the Koreish. He was then acknowledged the prophet by all Arabia. He died two years after his return to Mecca.

During the time he preached in the city, Mohammad had a number of close followers. Among his closest devotees were a few individuals who used to sit on a platform or "*suffe*" outside the mosque to listen to Mohammad's words and learn from his wisdom. Some of these Moslems became the first Sufis in recorded history, and over the years they spread out to form different centers of Sufism in various parts of Persia and neighboring countries. In the early days of Sufism, however, no attempt to formalize the Sufi religion was made. Sufism was a very reclusive religion and relied strongly on direct teacher to student contact. Most of its first followers left their homes and took to the mountains, deserts and peninsulas in search of solitude and closeness to God. They abandoned the physical comforts of the material world and set off to pursue in silence and prayer a true cognition of God. Their ultimate goal was to transcend worldly life and reach an eternal celestial tranquility in union with God.

The devotees who sought this transcendence and solitude were closely emulating the Prophet Mohammad. The Prophet's first vision came to him in the seclusion of a cave in the mountain of Harra where he had increasingly been spending his time in prayer and meditation. During the Prophet's lifetime, his followers carefully transcribed the words and visions of Mohammad by writing on the skins of camel humps (Mohammad himself did not know how to write). In 645 A.D. (or 23 A.H.), which is about ten years after Mohammad's death, Imam Ali, Mohammad's brother-in-law and other religious leaders collected together all these transcriptions, collated them, and created the book of the Koran, with 114 chapters, 6,236 verses, and 77,439 words. This became the Holy Book for all followers of Islam.

The Morshed

Sufis hold the belief that, in addition to the guidance offered to them in the Koran, they must receive instruction and help in their quest for spiritual purification from a wise and experienced "master" or guide. Two words can be assimilated to denote these relations: *salek* signifies the aspiring devotee or follower of Sufism and *morshed* means the master or guide. Other synonyms of morshed include *Ghotb*, *Agha*, and *Pir*. These titles will occur in the names of various eminent Sufis discussed throughout this book. The morshed's superior knowledge and wisdom enable his role as leader. His example leads his followers to a greater cognition of God.

> "If you are a man of faith and deserve ascendence,
> The knowledgeable and wise Pir will take you as far as
> Allah
> Through witnessing and reasoning."[1]

A morshed, ideally, is an individual who is totally and inseparably devoted to God. He has progressed to a point of infinite awareness where he sees nothing but God. Effectively, he has lost all sense of "self" and has become one with God. The state of passing away from (or transcending) the self is known as *"Fana,"* which is succeeded by *"Bagha"*—the consciousness of survival in God. Thereafter, the morshed reaches the stage of *"Ghena"* or contentment, about which the Prophet has said: "Contentment is an imperishable treasure." The ultimate honor for a morshed is to reach the stage where he acts as God's caliph on earth; God's voice in the Koran says: "We have appointed you as our caliph on the earth."

The Salek

So much for the master or morshed - what of the aspiring salek? What are the prerequisites for becoming a Sufi? The first step in this search towards true cognition is a mental renunciation of the physical and material distractions of the world. The salek must realize the limitations of the five senses; he must understand that his senses may mislead him and that he must rely on his heart to lead him intuitively to the truth. Curiosity about man's origins and his Creator as well as a willingness to pursue true cognition of God through discipline, self-knowledge and prayer are two important qualifications. The words of Mohammad, "He who knows himself shall definitely know his God," promise attainment of true cognition. Willingness of the salek denotes the determination and integrity to pursue single-mindedly this search.

As well as a combination of curiosity and willingness, a salek must have a strong faith in the master who will act as his guide. To symbolize this faith and to mark the event generally, a salek takes with him five things when he first meets with his morshed. The tradition of presenting the morshed with these objects exists in many (though not all) of the different branches of Sufism.

1. **A shroud:** a piece of white material that will cover the whole body, as used by the Moslems to wrap the dead. When the salek wears this in the presence of the morshed, it signifies symbolically that he has given up his self-will, that he is as good as dead.

2. **Rock candy:** made of pure sugar, with a crystal-like appearance. The candy implies that the chosen path is a very sweet one.

3. **A coin:** a specially minted religious coin symbolizing the salek's dependence on the grace and kindness of the morshed even in worldly concerns.

4. **A walnut:** a symbolic representation of the salek's head.

5. **A black belt:** called a *zonnar*, this belt is a black cord of 40 black threads held together with 40 knots; it measures 110 cms

in length and signifies that henceforth, the salek will be obedient to the discipline of Sufism.

Ablution

Before the salek meets with his morshed, he is taken to bathe by an experienced salek, known as the *Pir Dalil* or guide. This process begins the special ceremony that marks the salek's entry into Sufism. The Pir Dalil waits outside the reservoir while the salek enters the water. After bathing, the salek is ready for ablution. There are several different kinds of ablution in Islam for different purposes. In this case, the salek will undergo the "ablution of repentance" wherein repentance from past sins occurs and preparation is made for a new way of life. All parts of the body are washed carefully while simultaneously praying to God. The Pir Dalil gives the salek instructions as to which prayers he should recite; while the salek is reciting, the Pir Dalil says a special prayer for him. The prayers of the salek (which express repentance) are then repeated with the Pir Dalil. Special attention is also paid to the order in which different parts of the body are washed.

The salek dons his white "shroud" after the ablution and is instructed by the Pir Dalil on how to behave when meeting with his morshed. For instance, when the salek is taken to the morshed, he must cross his arms in front of himself so that his right hand reaches his left ear and his left hand reaches his right ear. This gesture is called *Gol Bang* in Sufism and signifies that the salek admits total annihilation before the morshed as well as being prepared to obey all the commands of his master. Following this ritual, the salek seats himself cross-legged on the floor in such a way that his knees touch those of his master. At this point, the morshed teaches the salek a certain word (or *zekr*). Occasionally, special instructions are given, explaining, for example, the way that the salek should move his head or breathe while reciting his zekr. After a period of time, the salek's zekr instructions (if any) are changed and he is given new orders at a different meeting. This is one of the ceremonies of the *Neamatollahi* and *Khaksar* branches of Sufism. Each of the branches has an induction ceremony: the new salek usually celebrates with others. A special meal is cooked, known as *Dig Joosh* ("*Dig*" meaning large pan and "*Joosh*" meaning to boil).

The Khaneghah

The place of worship where Sufis gather is called the *Khaneghah*. This word is a combination of two different words: "home" and "time." (Sufis believe that the only period of their life which "counts" is that which is spent in God's service; and the time spent in the Khaneghah is spent for God - hence the name.) A Khanegah does not have any particular or distinctive shape; the walls, however, are invariably decorated with pictures of the Prophet Mohammad and of Imam Ali, and bear beautiful inscriptions in Farsi and Arabic; the most common inscription is: "Ali is Almighty." Imam Ali appears especially on the walls of a Khaneghah frequented by Shiites since he is the first Master of the Shiite sect.

"Circle of Zekr"

In addition to the personal zekr one gets, there are zekrs (or chants) that can be done in a group. There is a special ceremony which takes place in the Khanegheh, called the *Circle of Zekr*. The worshippers all sit in a circle on the floor, with their knees touching. The master of the sect is also present. The followers close their eyes while he begins to pray; then they repeat in unison one word, the zekr, while moving their heads from left to right and right to left. The word is chanted in harmony and uninterruptedly; it is usually the name of Imam Ali "*Ya Ali,*" or "*La-Elaha-Ella-Allah*" making a continuous and harmonious sound. The zekr is usually repeated one hundred and ten times; the number being a symbolic representation of the name "Ali" in Abdjad letters.[2]

The Khergheh

The last concept with which the reader must become acquainted before looking at the practice of the religion in detail is that of the Robe or *Khergheh*. This is a woolen garment worn by the morshed of a particular school of Sufism, a tradition which dates right back to the time of the Prophet. According to Hajviri,[3] Attar Neyshapouri[4] and Sheikh Mohammad Ghader Bagheri,[5] the first recipient of Mohammad's Robe was Oveys Gharani (whose story will be given in the course of the book). The "Original Robe," as it is known, is thought to have passed down the generations from the Prophet Abraham to Mohammad, to Oveys Gharani, and so on.

There are, in addition, many other Robes or Kherghehs which are given by the masters to chosen followers. These include the *Khergheh of Tabarouk*, (the Robe of Grace), and the *Khergheh of Tark* (the Robe of Abandonment of Temptation). The color of the Khergheh signifies the present position or the stage the salek is travelling in. For example in the stage of "Fana," the salek wears black Khergheh.

The passing on of a Robe is always marked with a special ceremony and the succession of masters within a school of Sufism is also determined by the passing on of a Robe (and sometimes also by a written letter of "permission" given by the master to his follower). The different schools of Sufism take their names from the main master who founded that school - hence the "Oveyssi school of Sufism at Karaj" is named after Oveys Gharani, the man to whom Mohammad gave his Robe.

It is possible that a Sufi master may have had many masters, but he will usually only be granted permission to teach by one of them. Infrequently, it happens that a learned person possesses such a high degree of spiritual and intellectual ability, that he is given permission to teach by every one of the masters of Sufism in his time. On such an occasion, all the different branches of Sufism unite to take that one master's name. This has happened a few times in the history of Sufism; a notable case is that of Sheikh Najm-aldin Kobra Khivaghi, born in 540 A.H. His spiritual attainment was so remarkable that although he was from the Oveyssi school, all other branches of Sufism at that time bore his name also. His school is now known as the school of Oveyssieh, Kobravieh. Any school of Sufism is called a *Tarigheh* - this is simply the general name for a school of Sufism; the particular name of a particular school derives from the great master with which the school has chosen to affiliate itself.

A master will usually choose his successor in the course of his lifetime and will pass his Robe on to him; sometimes he will write a letter of permission to his follower. An example (in translation) of one of these is given below. After praising God, His Prophet Mohammad and his followers, the letter goes thus:

> "As God commands that 'the heritage should be given to the heirs', and so the great Mirza Abol Fazl, the spiritual son, the father and the leader of Knowledge, has received my teaching and has been given a zekr, with God's permission. And manifestations, names, visions and essence have resulted; the seven lights of his heart and manifestations of his hidden lights have been seen in the presence of hidden witnesses; therefore I, Hossein Dezfouli Zahabi, have been instructed by Masharegh Vallayat (literally "the place of the rising sun of guidance" - refers to the great Imam Ali) to appoint on the Thursday night of Shaaban 12/1306 Hejirat this man as Caliph of the schools of *Ela-hieh, Khatmieh, Alavieh, Razavieh, Zahabieh and Einieh.* His duty and his responsibility is to teach and advise the people, and to help them to cognition." [6]

The letter ends with the master's seal and his signature; the original is reproduced below.

بسم الله الرحمن الرحيم

الحمد لله على ... والصلوات تسليما على قبلة الواحد و ... وجه

صاحب لواء الحمد والمقام المحمود والله انا ما ش خلفاً الملك
المعبود چون بحكم ان الله يأمركم ان تؤدوا الامانات الى اطلاق
... خبر معتبر لان لفيدنك الله لان رحلا واحداً يهدي
الله ما تطلع الشمس عليه وتغرب عنها مستظهار نقله العلم بجل
اسوة الكاملون المحقق في الاول والمستقبل نور من الموحد
زبدة العرفاء الاصفيا ابو الفضائل من زيد وقفاً اما الميرزا
ابو الفضال دام الله بركات انعامه الشريفه بمحمد وآله داعيا
وامنضايا تعريف الحج بنعمتارخ قضا مشرف ... دنيت
محب وللغير ذكر حق مشرفاته الطا نا لله ... بعنا
... ونتايج مستحصله و محصولات محققه از مخلياتِ انا لي
واسمالي وامعك وذاتي حاصل عنه وعزا نا طوام
... نوارجه ما طوار مسنع قلسم وجم مخلبات ابواعظم
الاود حضور ما اهد سعتده خلق كرله دزنع ج
دوارده مع شعبان المعظم ۱۳ النها م فتح رحم العم رحم
اللهبي الموحد ارزنا وولايت مسلوك لا الله عليه انا
ابتارت بهغير اختيار سطاه درخلاف وعطيه سللي
عليه الحمه حتميه عليه رضويه ذهبيه عتنه رمضان
اب بنصب جليل سفتودي ورموده و ضيفه المزر
از پار انقار و واتت يفضلت ونصب حلق واحل
سعيت طلباله وللغير تشكان كيفقه تعامل مدل
                                          حررة الفقير

Chapter 2

Sufi Theory
and Terminology

This chapter will have three main parts to it. First, we will have a short comment about Sufi literature. Secondly, we will have an explanation of twelve of the most fundamental concepts or principles of behavior that one finds in Sufi literature and conversation. Thirdly, we will look at the 40 stages of development for the Sufi.

Literature and Practice

In the fifth century A.H. (12th century A.D.), the great Sufi Abol Ghasem Ghoshairi classified and defined many of the key concepts of behavior in Sufism in a clear and comprehensive book known as "Ghoshairi's Treatise."[1]In the sixth century A.H. (13th century A.D.), Abu Hamed Ghazali, the famous Iranian philosopher and Sufi, brought out another book on Sufi theory and terminology, called *Ehyae Olom Din*.[2] Following these two major works, many of the great masters of Sufism have in turn set down and described their interpretations of Sufi theory. Chosen quotations from many of these masters will be used to illustrate and explain the fundamental points of Sufi theory.

It will be helpful to remember that in the terminology of Sufism, there are certain words with very precise meanings; words which are elusive without explanation. Almost all of these words are from the verses of the Koran. The difficulty lies in the fact that the Koran uses ordinary, apparently everyday words to express an underlying, metaphorical meaning that is not immediately obvious or accessible. It is necessary to be able to interpret the inner meaning of these words in order to understand the Koran on a level much deeper than the purely literal. Obviously, it is impossible to give an absolute definition or explanation of these words. Scholars have argued for centuries about the finer nuances of their meaning. Many of these words relate, directly or indirectly, to particular stages in the spiritual development of the Sufi, and to his relationship with God. A brief example should serve to illustrate the semantic point: the word "wine," used in poetry and prose alike, refers not to the liquid but, metaphorically, to the essence of one's being; "winery" denotes the Sufi's heart, or the essence of his heart-felt existence; the word "wine bearer" is a reference to God, who symbolically pours wine into man's heart, and gives him life. Thus one can understand the line "Your Creator will give you pure wine" (Koran, Sura 76-21).[3] The image has passed from the Koran into the poetry of the Sufi masters, where it holds the same metaphorical meaning:

"Pour the wine from the divine cup
Into the cups of your heart." [4]

"Oh God, all other men are drunk with wine:
The wine bearer is my fever:
Their drunkeness lasts but a night,
While mine abides forever." [5]

Shah Neamatollah Vali speaks of God and his followers as:

"a wine bearer and one hundred thousand cups."

One should be aware that the Sufi ultimately seeks to develop his spiritual practice and free himself from worldly attachments until attaining gnosis or a union with God. This experience is much greater and more lasting than any physical pleasure (such as food, sex, etc.) that one will experience in their normal life.

Therefore, attachments that tend to make the ego strong or divert the Sufi from his path of spiritual development are frequently spoken of as the "devil" or "evil" and, of course, one can easily create so many physical attachments that they create their own "hell on earth". If a follower, even though he knows better, allows himself to develop an attachment for a physical pleasure, it can be viewed as a "punishment of God" because, although he enjoys one of nature's great pleasures, it has now become another attachment that the follower has to overcome. You can say that it would be better for a Sufi to have pain than pleasure. The reason is that one becomes attached to pleasure while pain is, relatively speaking, an easier experience to forget or transcend. For this reason you will constantly hear masters tell students that if they have to desire or want, they should desire hardship instead of great pleasure.

The masters caution against the obvious and the not so obvious attachments. An example among the latter is the attachment to becoming a "great spiritual person."

The word "God" in literature can also be very confusing. It is something that can only be experienced or understood when one achieves a state of being that is sometimes referred to as "union with God". Common man, philosophize as he may, can not understand God with words and can only be directed along the path of development that leads to the understanding. To do this you need someone that can see you from the outside and tell you about your attachments and problems (which is why you must have a living master). As one purifies oneself along the path, one begins to feel what can only be described as a strong emotion closely related to love. Consequently, you will hear teachers exhort their students to keep and develop their "heartfelt love of God".

Sufi literature and Sufi people (including translators) can also be misleading, just as some well meaning followers are in all religions. You will find in some literature or from some students, discussions of God and the Devil as though they are physical objects, etc.

It is up to *you* the reader and beholder to sort right from wrong and this is inescapabily a part of everyone's development or practice.

Bearing in mind, then, the complications surrounding the inner meanings in Sufi terminology, we may now consider the following fundamental concepts through the words of some Sufi masters.

Obedience *(Ebadat):*

Ebrahim Adham, a great Sufi of the second century A.H. and a disciple of Habig Raie, speaks thus: "Free yourself from desires for both worlds, and keep only the Almighty's love in yourself. Do not let this world or the other (eternal) world find its way into your heart, but keep your heart toward God."[6] According to Ghoshairi's Treatise, obedience consists in a true sense of being subject entirely to God. The two worlds refer to to the earthly and eternal worlds (i.e. the physical and spiritual worlds).

Devotion *(Ekhlas):*

Ebrahim Adham says: True devotion to God is to seek only God and to be obedient to Him in every way and act.[7]

Obstacles *(Hejab):*

To quote Ebrahim Adham:[8] "The salek should overcome three obstacles, so that the door of happiness and richness may be opened to him:

1. Even if he is given the Kingdom of the two worlds (earthly and eternal), he should not become happy, because as soon as man becomes happy, he becomes greedy.
2. If he owns two worlds and they are taken from him, he should not become sad, for it is [only] a mortal happiness and desire that he is losing.

3. A man should not be deceived by the praises and gifts of others, for if he is deceived by what people give him, this means that his will is weak."

Prayer *(Dua)*:

The Koran says: "Pray to Me and I will answer you." Ebrahim Adham has been quoted, when asked why God did not answer one's prayers, as saying: "You know God but you do not know how to worship him; you know the Prophet, but you do not follow its instructions; you eat God's Affluence, but you do not thank Him; you know that Paradise is in store for those who follow Him, but you do not try to reach it; you know that Hell is established with all its fires for those who disobey God, but you do not try to avoid it; you know that the Devil is an enemy, but you do not show enmity toward him. You bury your father and mother but do not learn the lesson. You do not see your own wrongs, but you criticize others. With all these [sins] in front of you, how do you expect God to answer your prayers?"[9]

Trust in God *(Tavakkol)*:

The Koran says: "Trust in God for God is everything for you." Abu Torab Nakhshabi (3rd century A.H., a disciple of Abu Shaghiq Balkhi) has been quoted as saying: "Trust means that you must immerse yourself in the sea of obedience and keep your heart with God. If you are given something, you must give thanks, and if you have it taken away from you, you must be patient."[10]

Satisfaction *(Reza)*:

The Koran says: "God is well-pleased with them and they are well-pleased with God." Abu Torb Nakhshabi Sufi of the third century A.H. says: "Man will never satisfy God while he carries even the slightest liking for the world in his heart."[11]

Satisfaction, or *Reza* is one of the most important concepts in

Sufism. The Koran states that there are four states of a man's soul: first, a state wherein he is subject to the power of the Devil; second, a state wherein he has overcome this power through his obedience to God; third, the state of satisfaction, as referred to above. This is the last and most important state of the soul prior to reaching union with God - which represents the fourth and ultimate state.

Unification (*Touhid*):

The Koran says: "Say that there is no god but the Almighty God, then you will be saved."

Abu Abd-allah Khafif Shirazi, of the fourth century A.H., says: "Unity with God is reached by shunning all worldly desires."[12]

Cognition (*Marifa*):

Oveys Gharani, the founder of Islamic gnosis, instructs man to "Know your heart and protect it from all evil."[13]

The great Sufi master Shah Maghsoud Sadegh Angha Oveyssi elaborates the point thus: "It is cognition of God which frees man from all temptations, and strengthens his steps toward Heaven and toward his true self, until that time when he may begin to live the new and true life."[14]

Roozbahan Baghli Shirazi,[15] of the seventh century A.H., claims that there are three kinds of cognition: general cognition (which refers to man's cognition of the world around him), private cognition of the soul (which refers to man's insights into himself and his moods), and lastly, a cognition of the reality of God.

Sheikh Najm-aldin Kobra, also of the seventh century A.H., and a follower of Roozbahan Baghli Shirazi, speaks thus on the subject: "When you say that there is no god but the Almighty, and you truly cognize this truth, then your being will pass away into Mohammad. This is absolute cognition: gnosis will be absolute after the cognition of the truth of Mohammad, for Mohammad was the first Manifestation of God."[16]

Love and Beauty *(Esgh va Jamal)*:

Certain sufis believe that the worship of beauty, in all its forms, is an expression of love which will help man reach perfection; the physical appearance of an object is, according to them, a mirror which reflects and reveals the hidden qualities of that object.

Roozbahan Baghli Shirazi writes that "One of the characteristics of God is love. The self is in love with itself, therefore love, lover, beloved and the self are all one thing. Love is kindness, and kindness is one of God's attributes. Love and kindness are one and the same attribute in God."[17]

Rememberance *(Zekr)*:

Haj Abdol Vahab Naeini, of the 13th century A.H., states: "Rememberance is the farmer of the heart, the grower of humility and kindness, and the manifestation of wisdom."[18]

Fear *(Khushu)*:

Mohammad the Prophet once saw a man who was playing with his beard while praying, whereupon he remarked: "If he were truly humble, his limbs also would be humble."[19]

"Humility is having fear in one's heart; a sign of humility is that in prayer, limbs should be bowed to the order of God."[20]

Hope *(Raja)*:

Seyed Mohammad Noorbakhsh Ghohestani,[21] a 9th century A.H. Sufi, has given the following definition of hope: "Hope is the proximity of the heart to the grace of God, and the joy of the heart in anticipation of God's promises being fulfilled."

The above twelve principles of behavior are fundamental to an understanding of the basis of the Sufi belief. Each idea must be carefully understood and put into practice by the aspiring salek. These are not the only guidelines, however, which have been set out for him to follow.

The Forty Stages

The physical, worldly side of life holds little attraction for the Sufi, since the indulgence of vain desires will only distract him and lead him away from fulfilling his true desire: inner contemplation and cognition of himself and of God. The physical world is ridden with pain, suffering, disease and death; in contrast, the spiritual world of cognition is tranquil and everlasting. It can be said that to reach this stage of cognition and tranquility, transcending the pre-occupations of the everyday world, the Sufi obeys certain laws and disciplines and must pass through various stages of spiritual development.

Prior to the 8th century A.H., Attar drew up "the seven stages of the heart," or a description of the seven stages which a salek must pass through before achieving true self-knowledge and cognition of God. Later in the 8th century A.H., Seyed Ali Hamedani expanded these seven stages into forty. Since his treatise covers the same ground as Attar in greater detail, we will present a summary of it here. The reader should bear in mind the above discussion of general principles (some of which will be repeated in Hamedani's treatise), as well as the problems of specialized meanings ascribed to various Sufi words; problems which are increased in translation.

Stage 1: Willingness (*Nyat*):

If a sufi is given two worlds—that is, this world and all its wealth, and the next world, with its paradise—he should be willing to give this world to non-believers and the next world to believers. For himself, he should desire neither, but should keep only hardship and sorrow.

Stage 2: Concentration in God (*Enabat*):

Whether sufis are alone or in the company of others, they should see only God. To them, everything apart from God is futile.

Changes in the world will not distract their attention from God, and hardship will not lessen their affection for Him.

Stage 3: Repentance *(Touba)*:

All people who have eaten unlawful food must repent, and after they have repented they must not touch such food again because God will punish them. A sufi should avoid any food at all (whether lawful or unlawful) if he is in doubt about it.

Stage 4: Devotion *(Eradat)*:

People of the world want comfort, wealth and property; sufis want pain and hardship and the Almighty God.

Stage 5: Endeavor *(Mojahedat)*:

Most people endeavor to turn their tens into twenties; sufis strive to turn their twenties into nothing.

Stage 6: Contemplation *(Moraghebat)*:

Contemplation is a state of being with God, whether one is alone or with people. Sufis practice contemplation in order that God shall keep them from sin.

Stage 7: Patience *(Sabr)*:

If sufis suffer the calamities of both worlds, they do not sigh; if they bear the sorrows of both worlds, they do not do anything except have patience.

Stage 8: Rememberance *(Zekr)*:

Sufis have given their mind and heart to God in all circumstances. His name is on their tongue at all times and when help is needed, he is the only one to whom they give their voice.

Stage 9: Overcoming Passions *(Mokhalefat al nafs):*

For seventy years, a Sufi's nature and soul will want an easy life, but he will find only pain and sorrow.

Stage 10: Satisfaction *(Reza):*

Sufis remain satisfied with God even when they are hungry or without clothes. They do not step out into the road of free will, and do not walk except in the path of Humility.

Stage 11: Agreement *(Movafeghat):*

For Sufis, calamities and good health, blessing and denial are all one and the same. They are in agreement with whatever God gives them.

Stage 12: Submission *(Taslim):*

If Sufis become the target of all calamities and sorrows, or if they face death, they submit freely to the will of God.

Stage 13: Trust *(Tavakkol):*

Sufis live in a state of Trust. They never question God or other people. They see God, worship Him, and do not ask questions.

Stage 14: Devotion *(Zohd):*

Sufis possess nothing worldly. Their Robe and the command of God are worth more than everything else.

Stage 15: Obedience *(Ebadat):*

A Sufi's entire day should be spent reading the Koran and thanking God. All night, the Sufi should be standing to serve his God. His heart should be full of love for his master and his head full of his struggle for intuition.

Stage 16: Chastity *(Vara)*:

Sufis should not eat every kind of food and should not wear every kind of clothing. They should not sit with all kinds of men and their only search should be for the teachings of God.

Stage 17: Honesty *(Ekhlas)*:

Sufis must pray all night, and fast all day. If they should detect any disgrace in their worship, they should sell fifty years of worship for a glass of water, and give that water to a dog. Then they should say to themselves that their worship was not worthy of acceptance by God.

Stage 18: Truthfulness *(Sedgh)*:

Sufis take no steps forward except for the sake of God. With the rememberance of their master, their tongue speaks what is in their heart, and their heart informs them of the secrets of God.

Stage 19: Fear *(Khoaf)*:

Whenever Sufis think of God's justice, they fear God and they fear their master *(morshed)*. They never trust their prayers.

Stage 20: (which has no name):

The Sufi has no fear when he looks at God's grace. He is full of happiness and pride.

Stage 21: Self-annihilation *(Fana)*:

Sufis put their "self" into the melting pot of "fana" (pass into God or self-annihilation). They shun everything which is below God. Their tongue moves only for God and their heart moves toward God.

Stage 22: Permanence *(Bagha)*:

Sufis look to the right and see God. They look to the left and see God. In every state of mind, they are with God. They exist within Him and are satisfied with His forgiveness.

Stage 23: Certain Knowledge *(Elm al-Yaghin)*:

When the reality of certain knowledge occurs in a Sufi, he will see all of Heaven and all of the earth, and there will be no obstacle to his vision.

Stage 24: Has been lost during the course of time.

Stage 25: Gnosis *(Marifat)*:

Sufis cognize God through their knowledge of the worlds and of the Universe. They worship Him with all of their heart and have no doubt in their obedience.

Stage 26: Command *(Velayat)*:

Sufis have both worlds in their possession, yet all the grace of paradise is worth to them but a grain of dust.

Stage 27: Affection *(Mohebbat)*:

Sufis have all their affection concentrated in the one God Almighty. Their outer appearance and their inner self are one and the same.

Stage 28: Ecstasy *(Shouq):*

Sufi's body burns with the ecstasy and love for God, and his heart is rejoicing in God. There is no place left in his heart for the world and its attractions.

Stage 29: Unity *(Vahdat):*

Because the Sufi is absorbed completely in God, he does not belong to the world of materials, but to the world of Divinity. Wherever he is, God is with him, and he is with God.

Stage 30: Closeness *(Ghorbat):*

If a Sufi asks God to command the infidels to follow him, the King of the World will never refuse or object.

Stage 31: Familiarity *(Ons):*

A Sufi's familiarity is with God's name, his tranquility is with His message, and his way is to His Heaven.

Stage 32: Union *(Vesal):*

A Sufi's physical being is in this world, but his heart is with God. His body is on earth, but his heart is in Heaven.

Stage 33: Intuition *(Kashf):*

There is no barrier between a Sufi and God. If he looks down, he can see everything; and if he looks up, he can see Heaven. There is no barrier to a Sufi's vision.

Stage 34: Presence *(Houzoor):*

There is not a single moment when a Sufi is free from thinking about God and serving Him. There is not a single moment where he does not see God.

Stage 35: Dispassionateness *(Tajrid)*:

Whether a Sufi is sent to Heaven or to Hell, he still praises God. He is neither happy nor sad at the outcome of his fate. He never turns his face from the Beloved.

Stage 36: Individuality *(Tafrid)*:

A Sufi stands out from the rest of society and is alone in the world. If people annoy him, he is not distressed; and if people praise him, he is not deceived.

Stage 37: Exhilaration *(Enbesat)*:

If the King of Heaven sends His angel of death to the Sufi, he will yet not die until he has received the command to die from God Himself. He is not afraid of the angel of death, and thinks not of resurrection or of Heaven's angels: he sees only God.

Stage 38: Stage of being Overwhelmed *(Tahayor)*:

A Sufi is overwhelmed in God and calls out to Him; he is detached from other people and looks only for God.

Stage 39: Destination *(Nahayat)*:

When a Sufi reaches his everlasting goal and has suffered all the pains of traveling, then he will see God through his heart.

Stage 40: Gnosis *(Tasawof)*:

A Sufi is a man who has been purified of all desires, whose tongue is free from gossip and bad words, whose heart is free from bad influences, and whose eyes are free from all treachery. His eyes are closed to the two worlds, but are open to God. His soul is free from passion, and his words are pure.

These are the forty stages through which God's Messengers must pass. The first stage is that of Adam; the last is that of Mohammad: "Praise be to God, to Mohammad, and to all his descendents."[22]

This summary, though brief, should help the reader understand the difficulty of the path which a Sufi must follow. Only those rare individuals with great strength of character, with trust, and with faith as the guiding light of their heart will reach their goal.

Chapter 3

Influences and Origins

In studying the many and controversial interpretations of the derivation of the word "Sufi," one encounters extreme differences of opinion. A few of these opinions will be discussed here, starting with those which are apparently fallacious, and ending with the most probable interpretations.

Sufism and Sophism

The scientist Abureyhan Bironi contends that the Sufi system is basically related to the Greek philosophy Sophism, and that the word "Sufi" is a direct derivation of the word "Sophi." This has been an influential opinion for the many subsequent researchers of Islamic Sufism. Two significant points, however, should suffice to show why this opinion is probably wrong.

The first is a consideration of spelling differentation. In Farsi, the Greek word sophi is written with the initial Farsi letter "seni," whereas "sufi" is written with the Farsi letter "saad." Although these two letters share the same pronounciation, they are quite clearly two different letters. This point alone apparently invalidates Bironi's thesis. Even without considering this point, however, there is little evidence that the two words could be connected: sophism is a philosophical system of argumentation, usually intended to deceive through the use of a formal, and apparently correct presentation of an argument which is in fact specious; sufism, on the other hand, is a religious system based on Islam, which encourages the individual to search for inner cognition, for the truth, and for God. All forms of deceit, whether of oneself or of others, are automatically rejected. Islamic Sufism, furthermore, had no connections at all with any philosophy in the first and second centuries A.H.

A few lines of poetry, by Jalal-aldin Mohammad Balkhi, known as Molavi, dating back to the sixth century A.H., clearly shows the contempt that contemporary Sufis felt for philosophers and philosophy:

> "Philosophers of verbal reasonings have a wooden leg,
> And a wooden leg is not a firm pillar to walk with.
> The philosopher will not dare to speak the truth,
> For his heart has been sealed
> And so the truth will not be spoken through his mouth."

Another example, requiring a little explanation, can be found in the words of the Sufi poet Sanaei Ghaznavi, who died in 545 A.H.:

> "The man who is bound to illusory philosophies is not
> the man of true religion.
> Abu Jahl should not be called Abu Hekam."

Abu Jahl was a man who liked philosophy, and who lived at the time of the Prophet Mohammad. While he was known to most people as "Abu Hekam" or "the father of philosophy," the Prophet named him "Abu Jahl," or "the father of ignorance." Thus, Sufi rejection of philosophy can be traced right back to the very roots of the religion.

Taking into consideration the above lines of poetry, the differences in spelling of the two words in Farsi, and the great spiritual and intellectual disparity between Sufism and Sophism, it seems that one can dismiss Abureyhan's contention that the two are connected.

The "Wearers of Wool"

Another commonly-held belief about the origin of the word sufi is that it derives from the Arabic word "suf," meaning wool. Because the wearing of woolen clothing is part of an important tradition in Sufism, it is often thought that the appellation "Sufism" is correlated with their usage of woolen raiment; Sufis are thus designated as "wearers of wool."

The habit of wearing wool next to the skin dates back to the first masters or Imams of Islamic Sufism. They believed that physical bodily comfort would encourage spiritual lethargy; that the spirit, not the body, should be in command at all times, and that the body should therefore be kept in a state of submission and obedience to the spirit. But while this theory of the derivation of the word does have a foundation in the practices of Sufism, the words of Mir Ghotb-aldin Mohammad Angha provide a more intelligent perspective: "while every Sufi wears wool, not every person who wears wool (or "suf") is a Sufi." Along the same line, another theory contends that the word "sufi" is derived from the Arabic word "suffe" meaning "platform," referring to the platform on which Mohammad and the believers of Mohammad used to sit while worshipping God.

"Safa"

This brings us to the fourth, and most probable theory: that the word "sufi" is derived from the Arabic "safa," meaning honesty and purity. Since two major objectives in Sufism are the refinement of the spirit and the purification of the heart, this would seem to be the most accurate and consistent derivation. The practitioners of "safa" are called "sufis," meaning "good hearted," or "purifiers of the heart."

"Tasawof"

The last theory which will be mentioned comes to us from the great Imam Ali, the first Master of the Shiite sect. We have been discussing theories regarding the derivation of the word "Sufi" as it is connected with a follower of the religion Sufism. The word "Sufi" (a follower of the religion) is the same in both English and Arabic, but the name for the religion itself (i.e. "Sufism" in English) is different in Arabic. In Arabic, the word is *"Tasawof"*. Imam Ali provides the following explanation of this word. In Arabic, Tasawof is a combination of four letters, T, S, W and F. These are pronounced, respectively, Ta, Sa, Wo, and Fe. Each letter represents three words so that in consequence, the one word "Tasawof" embodies twelve concepts. These are as follows:

"**Ta**" represents:

1. *"Tark"*: to shun everything other than God Himself.

2. *"Toubeh"*: repentance.

3. *"Tougha"*: purification.

Thus, the first letter of the word enjoins the Sufi to renounce all physical desires and attachments which bind him to an earthly, transitory state.

"**Sa**" delineates:

1. *"Safa"*: purity and honesty.

2. "*Sabr*": patience.

3. "*Sedgh*": truthfulness.

The second letter of the word instructs the Sufi to be truthful in his heart and his words, washing away all thoughts until only those of God remain in his heart.

"Wo" embodies:

1. "*Wafa*": faith.

2. "*Werd*": rememberance of God.

3. "*Woud*": love.

The third letter of the word advises the sufi to be faithful to the path and direction which he has chosen. He should praise God and remember Him at all times, and the love for God should enlighten him and stay in his heart.

"Fe" represents:

1. "*Faghr*": poverty.

2. "*Fana*": to pass away in God, or to become one with Him.

3. "*Fard*": individuality. [1]

The fourth and final letter of Tasawof teaches the sufi to confess his nothingness, his "poverty" or his ignorance in the face of his God since only God is wise and knowledgeable. Furthermore, a Sufi must "annihilate" his self and pass into his master (or morshed). Since his master is truly devoted to God and has achieved true cognition, passing into the master is equated with passing into God.

The Origins of Sufism

Having discussed various theories about the origins of the words "Sufi" and "Tasawof," it is time to consider a few of the theories which abound as to the origins of the religion itself and the influences which may have affected its development.

There is a fundamentally important point to take into account about the origins of the religion. To begin with, there were very few Sufis in existence in the first and second centuries A.H.; and they lived for the greater part in deserts, leading solitary, hermit-like lives, far from the distractions of human contact; consequently, in these early years of Sufism, there could have been little direct influence on the first protagonists of the religion.

Furthermore, Sufis of that era were under strict instructions to protect their religion and to keep their internal affairs secret. They shunned all contact with the world and with their fellow-men; any exchange of ideas between a Sufi and a non-Sufi would have been regarded as a serious breach of faith. (Sultan Ebrahim Adham destroyed all of his written works by throwing them into the sea prior to his death, in order that they should not fall into the wrong hands; such was the importance at that time of preserving the secrecy of the religion.)

Over the years, as Sufism became more widespread, an exchange of ideas became more possible. There is a theory that the Indian Sufi Fakirs had strong influence on Islamic Sufism, and it is certainly possible historically that, at the time of the Mongol invasion in 700 A.H., their ideas did indeed spread among Islamic Sufis of that time. This theory rests on a similarity observed between the practices of bodily mortification found among both the Fakirs and a certain group of Sufis. Since the Indian practice has historical precedence, it is indeed possible that there is a connection between the two sects. It would be a mistake, however, to claim (as some have done) that Sufism is *actually derived* from this religion since, at root, Sufism was clearly free from outside influence.

Sufism and Christianity

The English orientist Nicholson provides a theory expounding that the roots of Islamic Sufism lie in Christianity. Nicholson's somewhat surprising argument rests in his observation of a historical similarity between the austerity of the lives of the Manavian monks and that of contemporary Sufis. While both Christian monks and Sufis have sought to distance themselves from the superficial attractions of the world, there is an important difference in attitude between the two sects. Whereas the Manavian monks withdrew into monasteries to avoid temptation, the Sufi did not need to abandon the world in such a physical sense; it was their practice to overcome their worldly desires by a mental process which immunized them from temptation to such an extent that their physical environment became an irrelevance. "One can be a Sufi even while sitting on a throne in a palace."[2] (Many of the famous men in the history of Sufism have indeed been kings.) Furthermore, the Koran expressly enjoins that monasticism should not exist in Islam (Sura 57:6). Nicholson's theory would therefore seem to rest on a somewhat superficial similarity of belief since the fundamental ideas of Christianity and Sufism bear little relation to each other.

Sufism and Buddhism

The last theory which we will consider here, by virtue of its influence on students of the history of Sufism, is that of the historian Ibn Khaldon, who contends that Buddhism has strong historical connection with Islamic Sufism. His thesis to this effect is largely based on two coincidences in the religions. First, there are some customs which are to be found in some Buddhist sects and in Sufism. For example, when a person sets out to leave his home to travel, he carries with him a satchel and a sea-coconut.

The second connection is that visions are used extensively in both Buddhism and Sufism. There is also similarity in that both religions have a king that becomes a great master: Ibrahim Adham and Gautama. To search for God, they have both left their palaces and searched until they found what they sought.

Ibrahim Adham's vision provides us with an example of visions:

> "My father was in Balkh," Ibrahim Adham is reported to have said, "and he was one of the kings of Khurasan. He was a man of wealth and taught me to love hunting. One day I was out riding with my dogs when a hare or a fox started. I pricked on my horse; then I heard a voice behind me saying, 'It was not for this thou wast created. It was not this thou wast charged to do.' I stopped and looked right and left, but saw no one; and I said, 'God curse the Devil!' Then I pricked on my horse again; and I heard a voice clearer than before, 'O Ibrahim! It was not for this thou wast created. It was not this thou wast charged to do.' I stopped once more, and looked right and left, and still I saw no one; and I repeated, 'God curse the Devil!' Then I pricked on my horse once more; and I heard a voice from the bow of my saddle, 'O Ibrahim! It was not for this thou wast created. It was not this thou wast charged to do.' I stopped and said, 'I have been roused! A warning has come to me from the Lord of the Worlds. Verily, I will not disobey God from this day on, so long as the Lord shall preserve me.' Then I returned to my people and abandoned my horse; I came to one of my father's shepherds, and took his robe and cloak, and put my raiment upon him. Then I went towards Iraq, wandering from land to land." [3]

Gautama (Siddhartha) was born just inside modern Nepal and was the son of a chieftain or petty King and was brought up in relative luxury. At the age of 29, he abandoned this life, his wife, and young son, and set off the discover the cause of human suffering and its spiritual cure. He became a wandering recluse and sat at the feet of various ascetics and teachers. [4]

Although Ibrahim Adham's life is undoubtedly of interest because it is so similar to Gautama Buddha's, it does not provide any conclusive evidence of a connection between the two religions, much less a direct cause and effect relationship. Other similarities, such as the shared belief in predestination are unfortunately not considered by Ibn Khaldon. Until such a time as new evidence is produced, or a new light is cast on the subject, it would seem clear that Islamic Sufism cannot be derived from the beliefs or practices of any other single religion.

The First Sufis

The roots of all branches of Islamic Sufism can be traced back to the time of Mohammad, to the 1st century A.H. (or 7th century A.D.). At that time, some of the first diciples of the Prophet Mohammad used to sit with the prophet outside the mosque on a platform (or "suffe") and spent their time praying (amongst whom Salman Farsi was the most prominent).[5] Hajviri, the author of *Kash al-Mahjoob* writes that one day as the prophet was passing by the people on the suffe, he saluted them and said "praise be to you and the people coming after you who are as fair as you are. You are my friends and paradise is your place."

Together, Mohammad and these people discussed the way to true cognition of God, and out of this emerged the ideas which form the basis of the religion which later became known as Sufism. As they talked, they attracted more listeners and disciples. They went off, in the course of time, to form centers of Sufism in different parts of the land. Thus, centers of Sufism were formed at Baghdad and at Khurasan in the 2nd century A.H., at Shiraz in the 4th century A.H., in Kurdestan in the 6th century, and at Karaj in the 14th century A.H. After a few centuries, the first three of these centers had more or less disappeared. In the present time, there are Khaneghahs all over Iran, but only two main centers of Sufism, one in Kurdestan and one in Karaj. The following chapters will explore both the ancient and modern centers.

The Centers of

Sufism:

Past and Present

Chapter 4

Historical Centers of Baghdad, Khurasan and Shiraz

The Center at Baghdad

The city of Baghdad, which is now the capital of Iraq, was once in Iran. In 132 A.H., The Abbasi dynasty (consisting of united Arabs and Iranians) overthrew the Imavi (Arab) dynasty, and created a new capital of the Islamic world in Baghdad. Junaid Baghdadi (died 298 A.H.) was, with three others, the founder of the first center of Sufism in Baghdad. His descendence is shown in the chart on the following page. The other three founders were Rovaim, Ibn Ata and Omar Ibn Osman.

One of the most influential and famous Sufis of the Baghdad center was Housain Ibn Mansour Hallaj (died 309 A.H.), younger contemporary of Junaid Baghdadi, and thought by some to be his follower. (The point has been argued by scholars for centuries and is merely offered here as a hypothesis.)

Hallaj was the first Sufi to be a martyr to his religion. He was accused of heresy for pronouncing the words "Ana al Hagh," meaning "I am God," thereby theoretically claiming divinity for himself. Insofar as he is perceptible through the cloud of historic

Mohammad the Prophet

Salman Farsi   Oveys Gharani

Habib Raie

Seri Seghati

Junaid Baghdadi
(nephew of Seri Seghati)

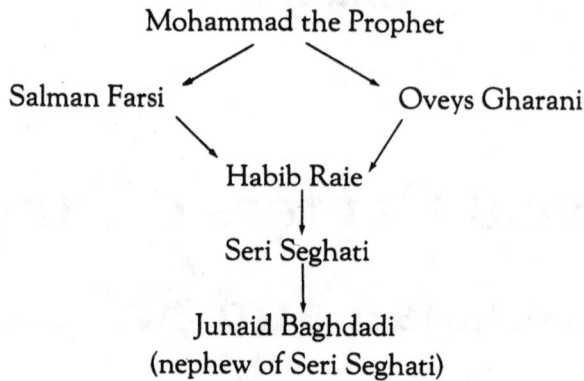

Junaid Baghdadi was also a follower
of Hares Mahasebi (died 234 A.H.).

polemic, he appears as a tragic and misunderstood worshipper of God. His intention, it would seem, was far from heretical. He believed that his spirit had actually passed away into God, and that the words spoken had come directly from God Himself, who had merely used Hallaj's body as a vehicle of communication. His poetry and sayings appear to exonerate him from the charges of self-divinization and pantheism which were levied at him:

> "Betwixt me and Thee there lingers an 'It is I' that torments me.
> Ah, of thy grace, take this 'I' from between us.
> I am He whom I love, and He whom I love is I,
> We are two spirits dwelling in one body.
> If thou seest me, thou seest Him,
> And if thou seest Him, thou seest us both." [1]

Hallaj's servant, Ibrahim Ibn Fatik, describes his crucifixion thus:

> "When al-Hallaj was brought to be crucified and saw the cross and the nails, he recited two prayers, and I was standing near him. He first recited this verse from the Koran:

'And I shall try you for good and evil, and you will return to me' (Chapter 29, verse 57).

Then he recited the verse beginning 'Every soul shall taste of death' (Chapter 29, verse 57); when he had finished reciting, he spoke some words which I do not remember entirely, but what I do remember went thus:

"...Oh my God, who art revealed in every place, and yet who art not in any place, I beseech Thee by the truth of Thy Divine Word which declares that I am, and by the truth of my weak human word which declares that Thou art, sustain me in gratitude for this Thy grace, that thou didst hide from others what Thou didst reveal to me of the glory of Thy countenance, and of Thy mystery.

"And these Thy servants, who are gathered together to slay me in zeal for Thy religion, seeking Thy favor, forgive them. For if Thou hadst revealed to them that which Thou hast revealed to me, they would not have done that which they have done; hadst Thou withheld from me what Thou hast withheld from them, I should never have been tried with this tribulation. To Thee be praise in all Thou doest; to Thee be praise in whatsoever Thou willest.

"Then he was silent. The Headsman stepped up and dealt him a smashing blow which broke his nose, and the blood ran onto his white robe. The mystic al-Shibli, who was in the crowd, cried aloud and rent his garment, and Abu Husayn al-Wasti fell fainting, and so did the other famous Sufis who were there, so that a riot nearly broke out. Then the executioners did their work."[2]

Many Sufis, following Hallaj, have believed that it is possible for God to manifest Himself in man, and to speak through the mouth of an ordinary mortal. They believe that if a man should utter the words "I am God," it must indeed be the voice of God speaking, and that this is the ultimate manifestation of the union between man and God.

After Hallaj was publicly scourged and crucified, there ensued a wave of persecution of the Baghdad Sufis. Nowadays, Hallaj and those like him are thought of as holy martyrs, whose only fault was that they revealed to others that which had been revealed to them.

The Center at Khurasan

Khurasan (which means "land of the rising sun") was once an immense province that stretched to the borders of India and as far as the Amau Doria mountains. Today, Iran retains the south-western part of this ancient kingdom, bordered on the east by the Hari Rud valley, on the north by a curving extension of the Alburz mountain, and by the river Atrack, which flows into the Caspian sea. At the center of Khurasan was the holy city of Meshed, which bears the tomb of Imam Ali al-Reza, the eighth master of the Shiite sect.

Meshed occupies the approximate site of an ancient town, Noqan, about whose history nothing is known except that it was the capital of the Tus district at the beginning of the Islamic period.[3] The founder of this center was the great Sufi Ibrahim Adham, who lived and taught there. His descendence is shown below.

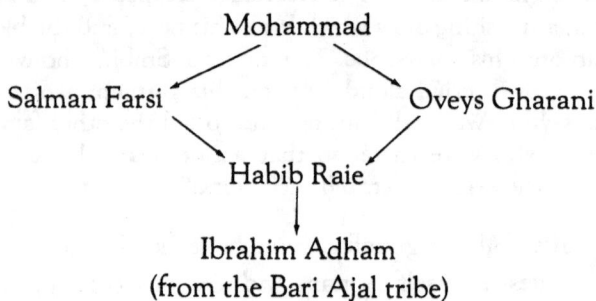

Mohammad

Salman Farsi   Oveys Gharani

Habib Raie

Ibrahim Adham
(from the Bari Ajal tribe)

(Contemporaries of Ibrahim Adaham were Fuzil Ibn Ayaz and Davoud Ibn Nassir Tae.)

Ibrahim Adham (died 160 A.H.) was born and raised in Balkh, a city in the state of Khurasan of which he later became king. The story of his conversion to Sufism runs thus:

"Ibrahim Adham was the king of Balkh. One night, when he was resting on his golden bed, with silken covers, he heard a voice coming from the roof of his palace. He called out: 'Who is there?' and a voice answered: 'A friend, looking for his camel.' Ibrahim accused him of ignorance, and demanded to know just what a camel would be doing on the roof of a palace. The voice answered him thus: 'You are the ignorant one, for you search for God while you sit on a gold throne and wear silken cloths. To search for a camel on the roof of a palace is no more strange than what you are doing.' This event enlightened Ibrahim Adham, and he abandoned his palace and his wealth in order to search for true cognition."

The first follower of Ibrahim Adham was Abu Ali Shaghigh Balkhi, who was martyred in 194 A.H. for being of the Shiite sect. The following story has been related about his life:[4]

On his way to Mecca, Shaghigh Balkhi stopped at Baghdad, where he met the Abbasi's caliph, Haron al Rashid, who asked him if he would give him some words of guidance. Shaghigh Balkhi replied by asking Haron what he would do if he were in a desert almost dying of thirst, and someone offered him a glass of water in exchange for half of his kingdom. Haron answered that he would give the man half his kingdom. Shaghigh Balkhi then asked him what he would do if, having drunk that water, he was unable to expel it from his body and was about to die, and someone came along and offered to cure him, for the price of the other half of the kingdom. Haron replied that he would give the man the other half of his kingdom. Shaghigh Balkhi then asked Haron "Why are you so proud of a kingdom which can be bought for a glass of water?" Haron wept, and thereafter held Shaghigh Balkhi in great respect.

Hatam Asam (died 237 A.H.) was a follower of Shaghigh Balkhi, and an unshakeable believer in the principle of Trust in God (*Tavakkol*). He was once asked on what rested his trust in God, and this was his reply: "On four principles: I have learned that no-one but me can eat my daily bread, so I know that God has provided for each of us; I have quieted myself with the knowledge that no-one performs my acts except me, so I am busy with them; I have learned that death will come suddenly, and so I run to meet him; and I have learned that I am never hidden from the eye of God wherever I may be, so I behave modestly before Him."[5]

Another well-known Sufi of the third century A.H. was Abu Yazid Bastami (died 262 A.H.), known as Sultan Bayazid, a disciple of Imam Mohammad Bagher (the fifth master of the Shiite sect). He was known as one of the "shattah" Sufis who were accused of blasphemy because of their sayings (see the story of Hallaj). Bayazid's contentious statement was "Praise me, Praise me, My Greatness is Imminent." A strong defense of Bayazid can be found in a book by Sheikh Farid aldin Attar Neyshapouri (who will be mentioned at the end of this chapter). Attar explains that when Bayazid uttered these words, he had in fact passed away into God, a state of self-annihilation known as *Fana*, and that it was God Himself who had spoken, not Bayazid. The same defense was made for many of the "shattah" Sufis, but they continued nevertheless to be accused by many of blasphemy and heresy.

Although there are many other famous Sufis from the center of Khurasan, we will consider only three more, all of whom expressed their devotion to God in striking poetry, excerpts from which will be quoted below:

The first of these is Abu Saiid Abi al-Khair (5th century A.H.), who, like Bayazid, was a "shattah" Sufi. He had many followers who would sit in a circle around him chanting. This was the origin of the ceremony known as the "Circle of zekr". Following are some of his quatrains:[6]

> "Thy sinful servant I Thy mercy, where now?
> In my heart darkness lies Thy comfort, where now?
> Obedience can win Thy Paradise - Why then
> A merchant there - Thy goodness, where now?

> "Long did we rest ere yet the arch of the sphere over the
>   void was flung.
> Long ere the azure vaults of the courts of Heaven
>   appeared.

In eternal non-being we slept secure and on us was
    stamped
The seal of Thy love, before we had known what it was to
    be.

∽✺∽✺∽✺∽

"I said to Him 'For whom dost Thy beauty thus unfold?'
He answered me 'For Myself, as I am I was of old.
For Lover am I and I alone the Beloved.
Mirror and Beauty am I Me in myself behold.'"

   Khajeh Abd allah Ansari (died 481 A.H.), known as Pir-Ansar (or
Master Ansar) is the author of a book on the Masters of Sufism,
Tabeghat al-Sufie. Following are some quotations from his prayers:

"Thou Whose Breath is sweetest perfume to the spent and
    anguished heart,
Thy rememberance to Thy lovers bringeth ease for every
    smart.
Multitudes like Moses, reeling, cry to earth's remotest
    place:
'Give me sight, O Lord!' they clamor, seeking to behold
    Thy Face.
Multitudes no man hath numbered, lovers and affected
    all,
Stumbling on the way of anguish, 'Allah! Allah!' loudly
    call.
And the fire of separation sears the heart and burns the
    breast,
And their eyes are wet with weeping for a love that gives
    not rest.
'Poverty's my pride' Thy lovers raise to heav'n their battle-
    cry,
Gladly meeting men's derision, letting all the world go by.
Such a fire of passion's potion Pir-i Ansar quaffing feels,
That, distraught, like Laila's lover, through a ruined world
    he reels."

∽✺∽✺∽✺∽

"Oh God, accept my plea,
And to any faults indulgent be.

Oh God, all my days have I spent in vanity,
And against my own body have I wrought iniquity.
Oh God, do Thou bless
For this is not given to any man;
And do Thou caress,
For this no other can."

∼∼∼∼∼∼

"Know that God Most High has built an outward
Ka'ba out of mud and stone,[8]
And fashioned an inward Ka'ba of heart and soul alone,
The outward Ka'ba Abraham did build,
The inward Ka'ba was by the Lord Almighty willed."

The last poet who we will mention here is Sheikh Farid Aldin Attar Neyshapouri. He first set out the seven stages which a salek should follow, which he called "the seven cities of love." The following verses come from his book of poetry *Mantegh al-Tayr*:

"The sun of my perfection is a glass
Wherein from Seeing into Being pass
All who, reflecting as reflected see
Themselves in Me, and Me in them, not Me,
But all of Me that a contracted Eye,
Not yet themselves, no selves, but of the All
Fractions, from which they split and fall.
As water lifted from the Deep, again,
Falls back in individual drops of rain,
Then melts into the Universal Main
All you have been, and seen, and done and thought,
Not you but I, have seen and been and wrought;
I was the sin that from Myself rebell'd,
I the Remorse that toward Myself compelled:
...Sin and contrition - Retribution owed
And cancelled - pilgrim, pilgrimage and Road,
Was but Myself toward Myself at my own Door.
...Rays that have wander'd into Darkness hide,
Return, and back into your Sun subside."[9]

Other poems in the book tell the symbolic story of the flight of thirty birds from the city of desire to the mountain Ghaf, where *"fana"* or self-annihilation is to be found.

The Center at Shiraz

Shiraz is a city in the state of Fars, and was, during the Achae-
menian period, the cradle of Iranian unity. Its dialect, Farsi, has
become the official and literary language of Iran. Historically, Shiraz is an important city; it gave birth to Cyrus, the great king of
Iran who is praised in the Old Testament, and is one of the cities
where one of the three kings who went to visit Christ when he was
born came from. Modern Shiraz is an important center for science,
literature and Sufism. The center of Sufism at Shiraz was founded
at the same time as the center at Khurasan.

The history of the city of Shiraz is open to different interpretations: some historians say it was built after the Arabian attack;
notably, Guyle Strange in his book "The Lands of the Eastern
Caliphate" claims that Shiraz, the capital city of Fars, was built up
by Moslems at the time of Omar, the leader of the attack; but
according to recent discoveries, notably those of Professor George
Gamaron of the University of Chicago, there are indications that
Shiraz's history begins *before* the Arabian attack. Professor
Gamaron has discovered some tablets indicating the wages of
labor workers who were building the king Daruish's palace in Per-
sepolis (known as Shiraz nowadays). This palace was built in 517
B.C., and the discovery of the tablets therefore provides interest-
ing evidence that the history of the city of Shiraz dates back to
long before the attack of the Arabs.

Islam influenced Iranian culture as much as Iranian culture had
influenced the Arabian caliphs after the attack of the Arabs: for
example, the fall of the Amavi (Arab) dynasty, brought about by
the Abyssinians, was helped by Iranian support. Furthermore,
under Iranian influence, the Arabian caliph Mansour changed his
capital city from Medina to Baghdad, which at that time was on
Iranian land. The Iranians put much effort into trying to influence
the Arabian caliphate with their ideas, while yet supporting the
Arab master Imam Ali and his sons.

P.K. Hitti, in his book *History of the Arabs*, discusses a group of
unsatisfied Shiites (followers of Imam Ali), who, under the leader-

ship of Ibrahim and his brother Mohammad (both great grandsons of Imam Ali) created considerable trouble for the Abassi caliphate; they were, however, finally destroyed by the Caliphate's army.[10]

In 876 A.H. (under the rule of the king Yacob Saffari), Shiraz became the capitol city. In 879 A.H., in the kingdom of Amr, Yacob's brother and successor ordered the first great mosque of Shiraz to be built. In 945 A.H., the Arab caliphates came under the rule of the Iranian Shiite dynasty known as Al-e Bu-ye. The king of this new dynasty ordered the Arab caliph Al Mostakfie to be overthrown, and from that time, the caliphate was called "Al Mottie," meaning "Under my Command."

Abu Abd allah Mohammad Khafif Shirazi (known from now on as "Khafif," for the sake of simplicity) was inspired to Sufism by the example of his mother. He was the master of several schools of Sufism; and the Oveyssi school was at that time named after him.

Khafif passed away in approximately 290 A.H. His mausoleum is in Shiraz, in a place called Darb-e Shah-zadeh, at the end of the Bazar Nov, close to the Bazar Vakil. It is considered a holy place by the many Sufis who gather there every Thursday to hold the Circle of zekr. Khafif is said to have performed many miracles in his lifetime, and even today, people still gather at his tomb and beg for help. He has left a legacy of over twenty six books; among his most quoted phrases are:

> "Faith is the heart's belief in what it receives and is taught by the invisible."

> "A Sufi is a man who wears *suf* (wool) through purity, and leaves behind him all desires and the whole world."

Sheikh Abu Mohammad Roozbahan Ibn Abi Nasr Baghli Shirazi was born in 522 A.H. (1128 A.D.) in Fasa, a suburb of Shiraz. He was known as a "Shattah" Sufi. Roozbahan, one of the greatest of the Oveyssi Sufis, wrote over 116 books, and had many great Sufis among his devotees: Sheikh Najm al-Din Kobra received the Robe from him.

Rooz bahan said in one of his books: "When I was three years old, I had a question in my mind as to where the God of all things

"Important Masters of Sufism in Shiraz"

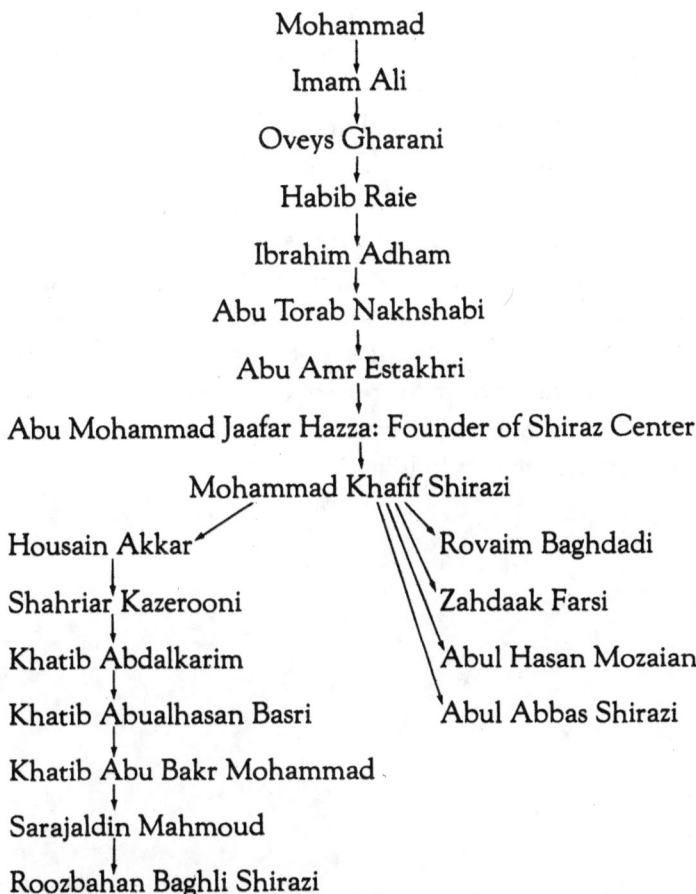

Mohammad
↓
Imam Ali
↓
Oveys Gharani
↓
Habib Raie
↓
Ibrahim Adham
↓
Abu Torab Nakhshabi
↓
Abu Amr Estakhri
↓
Abu Mohammad Jaafar Hazza: Founder of Shiraz Center
↓
Mohammad Khafif Shirazi

Housain Akkar	Rovaim Baghdadi
Shahriar Kazerooni	Zahdaak Farsi
Khatib Abdalkarim	Abul Hasan Mozaian
Khatib Abualhasan Basri	Abul Abbas Shirazi
Khatib Abu Bakr Mohammad	
Sarajaldin Mahmoud	
Roozbahan Baghli Shirazi	

could be found. Divine love settled deep in my heart when I was seven years old, and made me choose to pray and to seek solitude. And when I was fifteen years old, I became acquainted with the Secrets."

The first researcher to find the grave of Roozbahan was the Russian scholar Ivanov. He accidentally found a hand-written book of

one of the grandsons of Roozbahan, and through information con-
tained in this book succeeded in finding his grave. At present
time, that area has been re-built.

Another famous Sufi and poet holds a world-wide reputation
and Goethe was one of his devotees. He is Khajeh Shams al-Din
Mohammad Hafez Shirazi. He is also known to have been an
Oveyssi Sufi, and to have been the follower of Pir Golrang, who is
related to the school of Roozbahan.

He was born around A.D. 1320 in Shiraz, and he died in A.D.
1398. His tomb is located in Shiraz, and is called Hafezi-ie. The
word "hafez" means "one who knows the Koran by heart"; verses
of Hafez's poetry are loved and repeated by people of all classes.
People open his works at random and pick out passages, from
which the future is foretold. (It is not easy to convey the immense
respect that Iranians have for poetry and poets. Poetry is a central
part of the culture, and has traditionally been used to express the
most important subjects in Islam.)

Chapter 5

The Present Centers of Kurdestan, Karaj, and the Remaining Branches of Sufism in Iran

Center at Kurdestan

Located in the Southwestern part of Iran, the borders of Kurdestan lie from Khozestan to the Fani Valley. The people speak a Kurdish dialect similar to Phalavi, the language of ancient Iran. In the northern part of Kurdestan to Ravanfar, the people are of the Sunni sect. From Ravanfar on, the people are Shiite and are known as Ahl-e Hagh. The center at Kurdestan concentrates on worship through ceremonial rituals, some of which are practices unique to the center. Generally speaking, there are four groups of Moslems in Kurdestan, one of which is not Sufi and will therefore not be mentioned here. Of the three remaining groups, two are of the Sunni sect and one is Shiite. These two Darvish sects are illustrated below (Darvish denotes the adherent to a Sufi order):[1]

```
╔═══════════════════════════════════════════════════╗
║                Kurdestan's Darvish                 ║
║                                                     ║
║       Shiite Sect              Sunni Sect           ║
║          |                    /          \          ║
║       Ahl Hagh          Ghaderi-ie    Nagshbandi-ie ║
║          |                   \           /          ║
║       follower of          followers of             ║
║          |                    /       \             ║
║                              /      Ghader Gilani    ║
║       Sultan Es-Hagh        /                       ║
║                      Mohammad  Naghshband           ║
╚═══════════════════════════════════════════════════╝
```

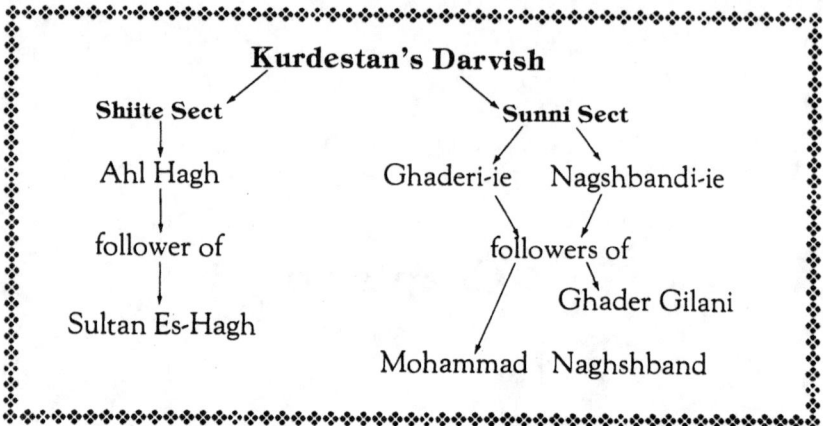

Sufism is not as old in Kurdestan as it is in other centers. It came to Kurdestan with the coming of Abd al-Ghader Gilani's sons to this district, from Baghdad, around the 6th century A.H. It is to the followers of Gilani that we shall now turn.

Ghaderi-ie:

These are the followers of Sheikh Abu Mohammad Abd al-Ghader Gilani. Abd al-Ghader was born in 561 A.H. (1166 A.D.), and passed away in 656 A.H. at the age of 95. His tomb is in Baghdad. His sons, first Abd al-Vahab, then Abd al-Salam and Abd al-Razzagh, were responsible for bringing this school of Sufism to Iran. At the present time, this sect has settled in Kurdestan and their Sheikh is Sheikh Ali Karkoki.

The branches of Ghaderi-ie extend beyond the borders of Iran to Iraq, Syria, and over to India. The Ghaderi-ie are well known for their very wild performance of a common Sufi ceremony called the Circle of Zekr. The Kurdish participants in this ceremony reach an extraordinarily high state of excitement: people swallow glass, push swords through their hands and necks, and sometimes even cut their necks. This sort of ceremony is known as "Tigh Bazi," meaning "sword play." They also perform ritualistic ceremonial dances.

The Ghaderi-ie are Shafei Sufis[2] of the Sunni sect; the ceremonies described above only appear to be practiced by the Ghaderi-ie of Kurdestan. It seems that they are able to reach such a pitch of hysteria that they are rendered immune to pain. As you can imagine, it is quite an astonishing spectacle for a newcomer. They are not only very strongly religious, but also rely heavily on the physical practice of ceremonies to further their faith. The following is a saying of Abd al-Ghader Gilani:

> "A salek should have four characteristics:
>
> 1. An accompanying knowledge that leads him to the true path.
>
> 2. An accompanying zekr which helps him in solitude.
>
> 3. A mind strong enough to prevent him from falling behind others.
>
> 4. A purity which will keep him from becoming attached to anything corrupt or unsuitable." [3]

Naghshband-die Darvish:

These are the followers of Sheikh Baha-al Din Mohammad Bokharaie Naghshband. He was born in 791 A.H. and his tomb is in the town of Ghasre Arefan in Bokhara. He wrote two famous books, one on Sufism, and one on ethics.[4] His genealogy will be found on the following page.

The following is a poem by one of the Naghshbandi's Sheikhs, Andalib Naghshband (A.H. 1199):

> "Since youth I've heard from Him, from afar.
> I have imagined that I held Him near.
> Now that I go to Him like a mirror,
> I see that this me is He." [5]

Naghshband-die

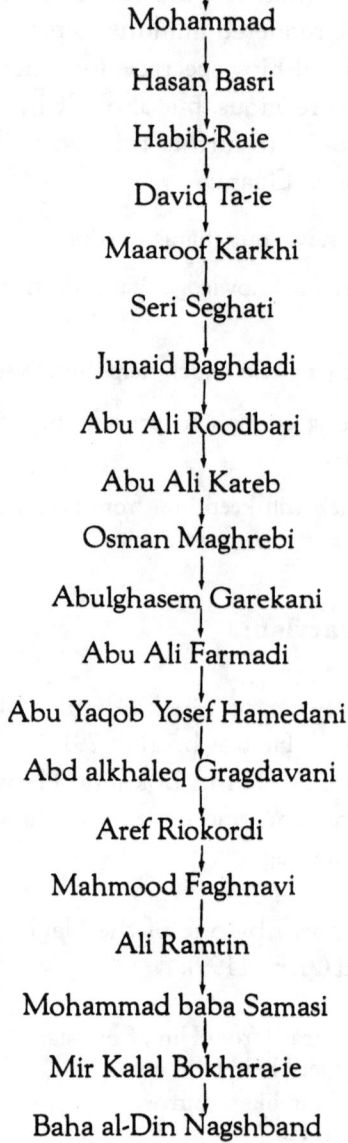

Mohammad

Hasan Basri

Habib-Raie

David Ta-ie

Maaroof Karkhi

Seri Seghati

Junaid Baghdadi

Abu Ali Roodbari

Abu Ali Kateb

Osman Maghrebi

Abulghasem Garekani

Abu Ali Farmadi

Abu Yaqob Yosef Hamedani

Abd alkhaleq Gragdavani

Aref Riokordi

Mahmood Faghnavi

Ali Ramtin

Mohammad baba Samasi

Mir Kalal Bokhara-ie

Baha al-Din Nagshband

Ahl Hagh Darvish:

The Ahl Hagh Darvish are spread out not only in Kurdestan but also in Azerbaijan (in the northwest of Iran) and in the north of Teheran. The Ahl Hagh Darvish (Or Sufis) are of the Shiite sect, and are devoted followers of Imam Ali. Because of this, they are sometimes known as Ali Allahi (Ali is God). They are also known as Khajevand. These Darvish believe that the Devil is an angel of God, and consequently never curse him. One of their more distinctive physical characteristics is their long and heavy moustaches, which they never shave off.

They are the followers of Sultan Eshagh (known as Sahak). He was born in 550 A.H., in the town of Zoor In Iran. He came to Oraman (in Iran) and settled in one of the villages in Sirvan, which is now called the Valley of the Sheikh (named after either the Sultan himself, or after his servant). These Darvish hold a strong belief in the reality of reincarnation. Sultan Eshagh did much preaching on the subject: he himself believed that the spirit of Imam Ali had been reincarnated in him; according to him, the spirit of Imam Ali's followers had been reincarnated in the bodies of his own followers, and, furthermore, every spirit would pass through 1001 bodies. Thus, through an endless cycle of reincarnation, the spirit of one master would pass to another, and Sufism would be endlessly perpetuated. He had seven immediate followers, to whom he gave holy names representing the past masters of whom they were reincarnations:

To Shah Abrahim, he gave the name of Imam Houssein (3rd Imam of the Shiite sect).

To Yadegar, he gave the name Imam Hassan (2nd Imam of the Shiite sect). ·

To Pir Moses, he gave the name of Ammar Ibn Yaser (one of the prophets, and Imam Ali's follower).

To Benyamin, he gave the name of Malek Ashtar (a devotee of Imam Ali and one of the commanders in the Seffin war between Imam Ali and Moavieh Ibn of Sofian).

To David, he gave the name of Meghdad (devotee of Imam Ali).

To Mostafa, he gave the name of Ghanbar (a Shiite who always accompanied Imam Ali).

To the only woman follower, he gave the name of Fatemeh (the name of Mohammad's daughter and of Imam Ali's wife).

The Ahl Hagh Darvish begin their chanting ceremonies with prayers. These always open with the word "Hu" (or God) and the worshippers invoke the mercy of Mehdi (the twelfth Imam of the Shiite sect).

The Center at Karaj

The present center at Karaj is located 30 kilometers northwest from Teheran. The Oveyssi school is in the region of Sufiabad, a further 6 kilometers from Karaj. Unlike the center at Kurdestan, the center at Karaj has evolved into an important center of learning, as well as of worship. It is currently the focal point for Sufis all over Iran, as well as for scholars from all parts of the world who wish to deepen their knowledge of Sufism and of its history. The author was able to spend some time visiting this center to observe its practices, and an account of his visit there will be found in the final chapter of this book. An account of its history and the important Sufis associated with its establishment will be given here.

Oveyssi-ie Darvish:

These are the followers of Oveys Gharani. As historical sources show, Oveys Gharani was honored with being given the first and original Robe from the Prophet Mohammad; he is consequently thought of as the founder of the religion (Salman Farsi, equally respected, is thought of as the co-founder). All the various branches of Sufism can thus be seen to trace back to him.

Oveys Gharani was the son of Amer,⁶ and was born in Najd, in Arabia. He dedicated his entire life to asceticism and piety. Of medium height, he was so slender in stature that he has been called "Shaarani," or "hair" in Arabic, indicating metaphorically that he was "thin as a hair." He is said to have been a camel herdsman, earning a living for his old, blind mother by feeding camels in the pasture, where he would spend entire nights preaching. Because of his duties to his mother, it is said that he never actually succeeded in visiting the Prophet Mohammad; but he had accepted Mohammad's religion in his innermost heart, and was a faithful follower.

Mohammad is said to have faced Yeman⁷ at times (where Oveys lived), and to have said "A blessing blows in from Yeman." People would ask him "Who lives in Yeman?", and the Prophet would reply "A man by the name of Oveys Gharani." Just before the death of the Prophet, he called for Imam Ali and Omar (the second caliph of Islam), and said "Take my Robe to Yeman and give it to a man named Oveys. He is a man of moderate heighth, and is slender (shaarani). There is a white mark on the palm of his hand and on his side. He has acted as mediator between three tribes and God." ("Mediation" in Islam means to intercede between God and a soul wishing to approach God and to beg His acceptance.) "When you see him, give him my blessing, and ask him to pray for my followers and to mediate for them, for many of my followers will be accepted by God through the mediation of this man."

When the Prophet passed away, Imam Ali and Omar removed his Robe, to take it to Oveys. Reaching Gharan (where Oveys

lived), they searched for him and found him preaching in the desert. They waited until he had finished his prayers, and approach-
ing him, asked to see the white marks Mohammad had described.
When he did so, they had no doubt that this was the man they
were looking for, and presenting him with the Robe, they gave
him the message of Mohammad. Oveys took the Robe and prayed
hard, begging God's acceptance. After doing so, he said "God has
granted me intercession for the tribes."

At the end of this story, Attar (in his book, *Tazker Al Olia*)[8] nar-
rates that Omar asked Oveys, "If you were so devoted to Mohammad, why did you never come to see him?" Oveys then asked
Omar, "Have you seen Mohammad?" Omar, of course, replied,
"Yes." Oveys then said, "You might have seen only his clothes. If
you have really seen him, tell me if his eyebrows are connected or
are far from each other?" Surprisingly enough, Omar had no
answer.

Oveys then asked if Omar considered himself to be a devotee of
Mohammad. Omar's reply was, "Yes." Oveys then said, "What
kind of a 'true friend' are you if you could watch those people
break Mohammad's teeth and never break yours in sympathy with
him?" And Oveys opened his mouth showing not one single
tooth. This famous story has been told by most of the learned
and great Sufis and by poets in both Arabic and Farsi. A famous
Arabian poet, Daabal Khazai has written:

> "Oveys is the one who can help us approach God.
> The day will come when he will be our mediator."

One of the Great masters of Sufism, Sheikh Najm al-Din Kobra,
has said "Oveys Gharani was the lover of eternal grace. Any heart
which does not beat in this way, or any breath which is not
breathed in this way, has never known the grace of seeing the
Beloved."[9] He has also said:

> "If God's kindness is his closeness, how can apparent dis-
> tance be harmful? And if God's mercy is far, what is the
> benefit of apparent closeness? Since such a great man as
> Oveys Gharani put the fragrance of life in his heart and

on the fire of desire, thus the divine fragrance reached the
king of the Universe, Mohammad; and he said 'the fragrance of God comes from Yemam.' Otherwise man is
blinded by the veil of ignorance and evil you and I do not
see the light, only those, whom the love of the lovers of
the Beloved will help. The veil of ignorance will fall from
their eyes and they will see whatever could not previously
be seen. This is the gift of the lovers of God to these men."

Molavi also recalls Oveys in his poetry and says:

"Prophet Mohammad says that the breath of wind,
brings the divine fragrance from Yemem.
The fragrance of Ramin comes from the spirit of Veys,[11]
So the fragrance of God comes from Oveys.
The strange perfume from Oveys and Yemem
Made the Prophet drunk with happiness.
Since Oveys left his finite being behind,
His earthly being became heavenly."

Mohammad, while passing his Robe on to Oveys Gharani,
bestowed praise and respect on others of his followers; amongst
whom Salman Farsi is especially notable. He is highly respected by
students of the Oveyssi school, and is regarded by them (to put the
matter simply) as the co-founder of the school. Mohammad himself once said of him "Salman is one of us."

Salman Farsi:

Salman Farsi's[12] father was from Badakhshan; his home town was
Jey, in a district of the Fars region called "Ardjan's meadow." In
that area, there is a spring to be found called "Salman's spring."
Ebne-Abbas, an Arabian Mohadeth (a person who translates the
sayings of the prophet or saints), has quoted Salman as having
said: "I am a man from Fars, and by my ancestry I was Zorastrian.
One day I went to church, and saw the Christians praying. I was
amazed by their actions, and stayed there until the sun set. I liked
their religion, but my father disagreed and imprisoned me. I ran
away in a caravan to the city of Sham; there I went to the pontiff

of the town. He welcomed me, and I served him. When he was dying, he told me to go to the priest Nasibain, and to ask to serve a certain priest. I went and served this person, and when he was dying, he told me that a messenger from Abrahim's sect would be coming to Arabia, and that the sign of the prophesy would be visible between his shoulders. His characteristics would be that he would accept gifts, but not alms or charity. When the priest died, I came to Medina in a caravan, as a servant of a Jewish person. There, I heard about Mohammad's appearance, and went to visit him. On the first night, I offered him a gift, and he accepted it. On the second night I offered him charity, which he refused. I saw the sign of the prophetic mission between his shoulders and I kissed it."

Hamdallah Moostoufi, author of the book *Tarikh Gozideh*, writes: "Salman, a servant of a Jewish person by the name of Osman-ibn-Ashhal, came to Medina. Mohammad bought Salman from Osman for forty golden rupies and three hundred date-palm trees, and gave him his freedom. (It should be mentioned that at that time, the buying and selling of slaves was very popular. Among those associated with the Prophet Mohammad were several individuals who had been bought by him, and had thereby gained their freedom.)

Salman Farsi was a follower of Mohammad's who was particularly close to him. After the Prophet's death, Salman remained faithful to the Prophet's family, and to the Shiite pontiffs; he was also close to Imam Ali. Salman's death has been recorded as being in 36 A.H.; he apparently lived for a very long time; some have claimed that he lived for two hundred and fifty years. Various sources indicate that his grave is in Baghdad and that it is a place of pilgrimage. His funeral service was conducted in its entirety by Imam Ali.

Djazari quotes Mohammad as having said that the mastership would pass to Salman' nation. Followers of Salman Farsi are known as "Oveyssis," after Oveys Gharani. (As explained previously, Iranian Islamic Sufism owes its origins both to Oveys Gharani and to Salman Farsi.) The connection between the two great men is to be found in the person of one Habib-Ebn-Salim

Alraei (referred to elsewhere as Habib Raie), who was a pupil of
Oveys, and received the Robe from him, and was also a follower of
Salman Farsi. For a complete genealogy of the Oveyssi school,
please refer to the following chart.

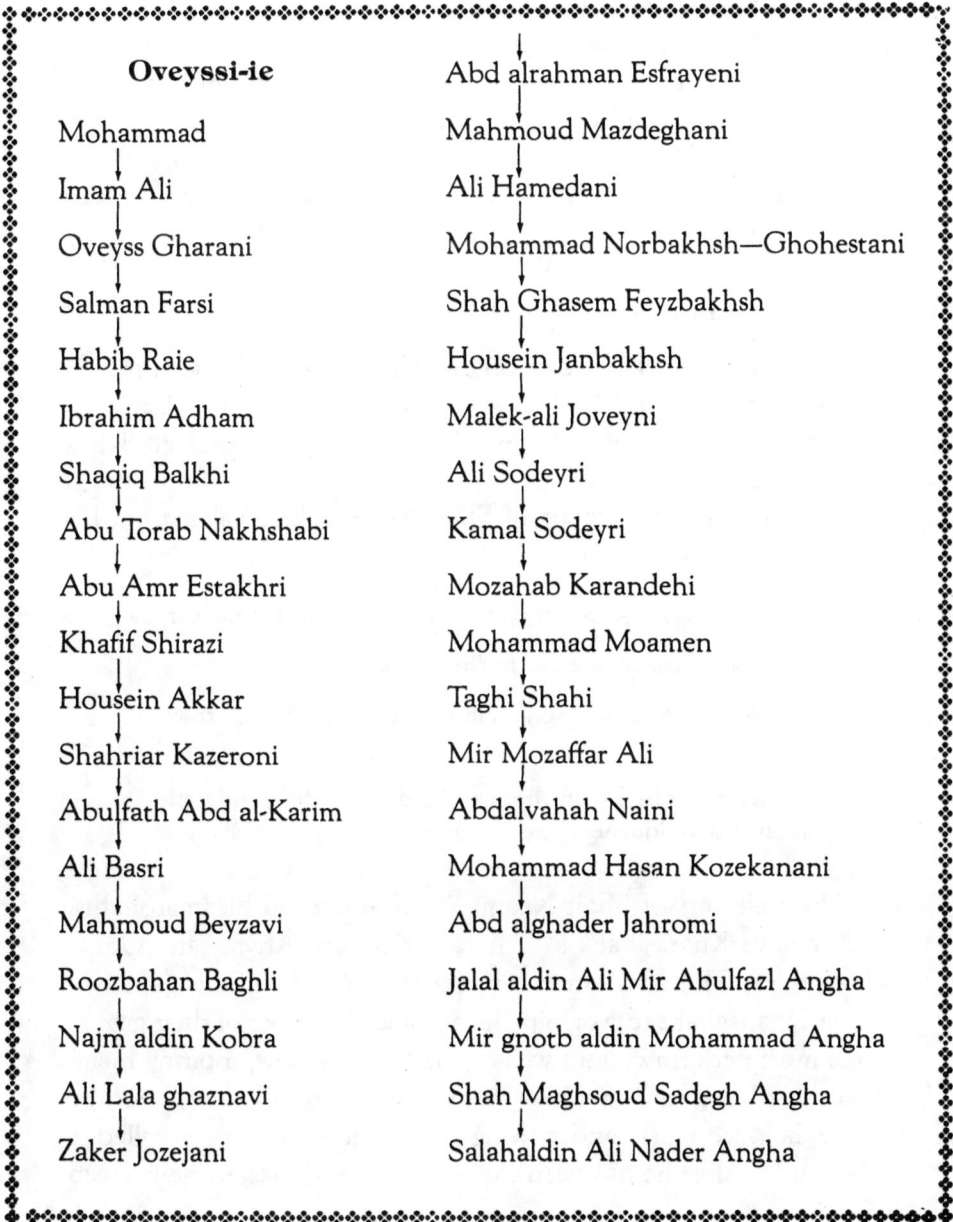

Oveyssi-ie	Abd alrahman Esfrayeni
Mohammad	Mahmoud Mazdeghani
Imam Ali	Ali Hamedani
Oveyss Gharani	Mohammad Norbakhsh—Ghohestani
Salman Farsi	Shah Ghasem Feyzbakhsh
Habib Raie	Housein Janbakhsh
Ibrahim Adham	Malek-ali Joveyni
Shaqiq Balkhi	Ali Sodeyri
Abu Torab Nakhshabi	Kamal Sodeyri
Abu Amr Estakhri	Mozahab Karandehi
Khafif Shirazi	Mohammad Moamen
Housein Akkar	Taghi Shahi
Shahriar Kazeroni	Mir Mozaffar Ali
Abulfath Abd al-Karim	Abdalvahah Naini
Ali Basri	Mohammad Hasan Kozekanani
Mahmoud Beyzavi	Abd alghader Jahromi
Roozbahan Baghli	Jalal aldin Ali Mir Abulfazl Angha
Najm aldin Kobra	Mir gnotb aldin Mohammad Angha
Ali Lala ghaznavi	Shah Maghsoud Sadegh Angha
Zaker Jozejani	Salahaldin Ali Nader Angha

The Remaining Branches

There are four "branches" of Sufism in Iran which are not large enough to be called "centers" in their own right, but which do each have their own Khaneghah.

According to various biographies and histories of Sufism, more than 20 branches have been recorded, but we will only deal here with those which gather regularly in Khaneghahs to pray.) Respectively, these four branches are: the Neamatollahi, the Maarofi-ieh, the Zahabi-ieh, and the Choshti-ieh, each of which will be considered below.

Neamatollahi:

These are the followers of Shah Neamatollah Vali (born in 730 A.H., died in 827 A.H.). His sepulchre is in the Mahan district of Kerman, in southern Iran. The chart below gives Neamatollahi's geneology.

The following is a saying of Shah Neamatollah Vali's, from his book Tahghiq (Research):[13]

> "The differences between things are due to their significances.
>
> Their significances are due to their qualities.
>
> The quality of anything is due to the uniqueness of that thing.
>
> Therefore things can be gathered and differentiated because of uniqueness."

The followers of Shah Neamatollah are called Neamatollahis. They have Khaneghahs in Teheran, Kerman, Ahvaz, and Gonabad. Every Thursday afternoon, the Neamatollahi Sufis gather in their Khaneghahs to worship. To become a member of their group, one must perform certain well-defined rites: a new, aspiring member must bring with him a walnut, a piece of rock candy, a coin, a rope belt (zon ar), and a long white cloak which is called a "shroud." After he has been introduced to his master, he is given his "zekr". These Sufis obey all the Islamic laws of prayer and fasting, and in addition, hold frequent chanting sessions, in which the poetry of Molavi is recited.[14]

Neamatollahi

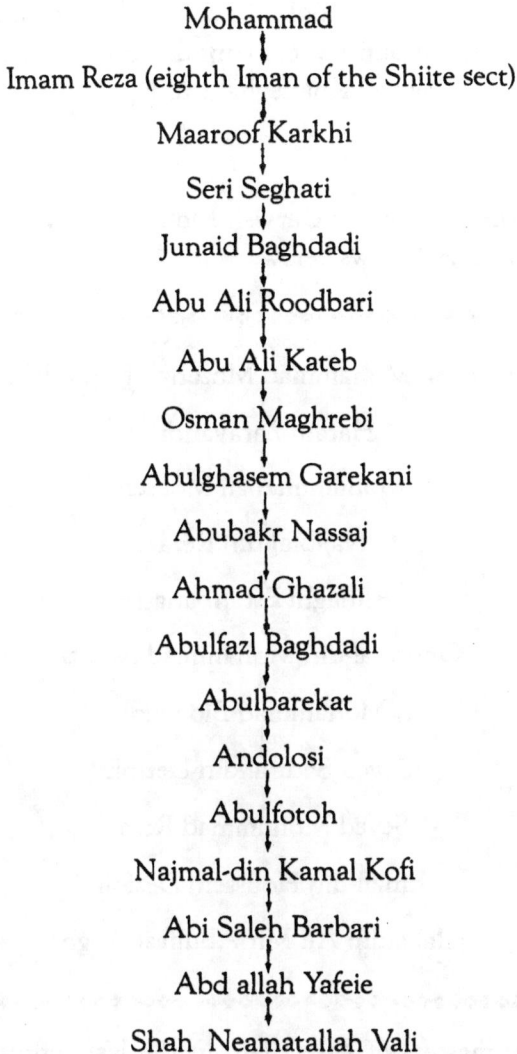

Mohammad

Imam Reza (eighth Iman of the Shiite sect)

Maaroof Karkhi

Seri Seghati

Junaid Baghdadi

Abu Ali Roodbari

Abu Ali Kateb

Osman Maghrebi

Abulghasem Garekani

Abubakr Nassaj

Ahmad Ghazali

Abulfazl Baghdadi

Abulbarekat

Andolosi

Abulfotoh

Najmal-din Kamal Kofi

Abi Saleh Barbari

Abd allah Yafeie

Shah Neamatallah Vali

Jalal al Din Mohammad Rumi Molavi was an Oveyssi student who had a great influence in Iran as well as on the various societies acquainted with Eastern literature and history. His poetry is known by heart by many of the Sufis in Iran. He lived his entire life in Ghonieh in Turkey, where he established a Khaneghah. He created a new method of chanting—the Circle of Zekr—which, after seven centuries, is still practiced in Iran and Turkey. Molavi is the author of *Masnavi*, a book of poetry which contains instructions on the ways of Sufism; it is considered a vital text, and is to be found in practically all Khaneghahs today.

Zahabiieh:

These are the followers of Darvish Mohammad Mozahab Karandehi. His genealogy follows below:

Darvish Mohammad Mozahab Karandehi
↓
Hatam Zaravandi
↓
Mohammad ali Moazen
↓
Najib al-din Reza
↓
Alinaghi Estahbanati
↓
Ghotb al-din Mohammad Neirizi
↓
Mohammad Bidabadi
↓
Seyed Sadr al-din Dezfoli
↓
Seyed Mohammad Reza
↓
Ein al-din Houssein Dezfoli
↓
Jalal-aldin Ali Mir Abulfazl Angha

One of the masters of Zahabiieh, in the last century, was Mir Einaldin Housein Mosavy Dezfoly, who is known as Zahir.

According to his own writing, he granted permission to join the religion to Jalal-al-din Ali Mir Abulfazl Angha Oveyssi. At this point, then, a connection was formed between the Zahabiieh and the Oveyssi school of Sufism. The actual handscript permission mentioned above is printed in a book by Abulfazl-Angha and is illustrated below. [15]

The following poem is one of Mir Einal-din Housein Mosavy's contributions to the literature of Sufism:

"Love is the Eternal King,
Love is N'* and a pen,
Love is the shining sun,
Love is the perfect flame,
Love is the endless light,
Love is the honor of nations,
Love is the hidden Secret,
Love is Eternal Angha,
Love is delightful sorrow,
Love is the brillance of light,
Love is the principle of cause,
Love is the Master of Heaven,
Love is a rich ocean,
Love appears as light,
Love is a valuable jewel,
I can see God in its light." [16]

Maarofi-ie:

These are the followers of Abu Mahfoz Maarof Karkhi, who was the follower of Imam Reza (eighth Imam of the Shiite sect). Their customs and genealogy are the same as the Neamatollahis.

---

*Note: The Arabic letter 'N' consists of an open circle with a dot at its center. The center point is usually interpreted as meaning "a thing created." The open circle is understood to "extend from infinity to infinity." In addition, the circular shape of the Arabic "N" symbolizes unity. The phrase "N and a pen" originates from a verse from the holy Koran. (The mystic "Pen" is one of the symbolic foundations of the revelation to man.) [17]

Choshti-ieh :

These are the followers of Khajeh Ahmad Abdal Choshti; they are connected to Adhami-ieh, as are the Adhammieh Sufis largely to be found in India. A chart of their genealogy follows below:

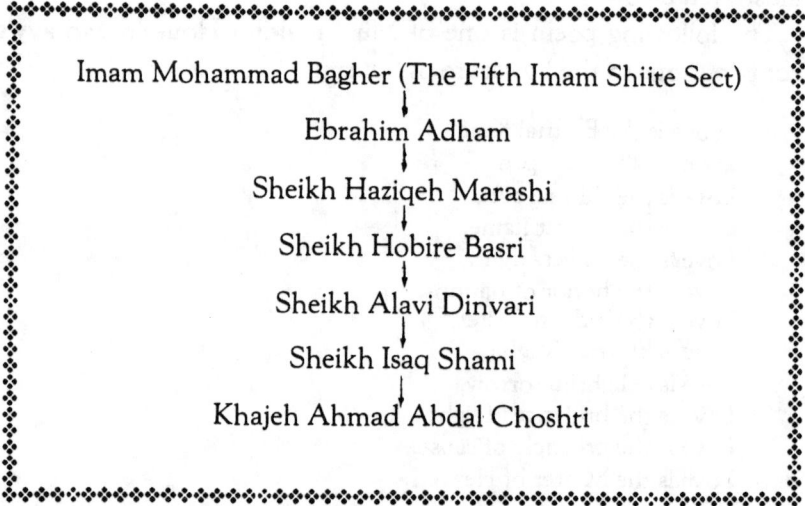

Imam Mohammad Bagher (The Fifth Imam Shiite Sect)
↓
Ebrahim Adham
↓
Sheikh Haziqeh Marashi
↓
Sheikh Hobire Basri
↓
Sheikh Alavi Dinvari
↓
Sheikh Isaq Shami
↓
Khajeh Ahmad Abdal Choshti

Moeinal-din Choshti, one of the Choshtiieh Sufis, who has written the following poem:

> "You are my companion, I do not want any but you.
> I do not long for anyone but you, who have attracted me.
> Secrets between us cannot be told to anyone.
> You know and I know, it does not need to be said.
> No one can settle in the palace of my life,
> No one is needed in my solitude but you.
> The ignorant wishes to have the world, the wise longs for
>   Heaven.
>
> I am the lover who lost his heart to the Beloved,
> And desires nothing but the Beloved.
> I do not drink wine, but since You are the wine-bearer,
> I do not want even one vein in my being to be sober." [18]

I will now turn to the detailed description of the Oveyssi School of Sufism at Karaj. The chapter will serve as a focal point by which you can understand the everyday practices of Sufis living today.

Tabarzn

Chapter 6

The Oveyssi School
of Sufism at Karaj

To become more acquainted with Sufi practices in detail, the author sought and was granted permission to visit with the Maktab Tarighat Oveyssi Shah Maghsoudi of the Oveyssi School of Sufism at Karaj. The center was actually located at 'Sufiabad,' near Karaj. From Teheran, one sets off to the northwest. After 30 Kilometers, a town is reached called Karaj, which has a population of about 30,000. This particular town is exceptional among small, agricultural villages, because of its pleasant climate and its produc- tive soil. It is also a recreation area for the people of Teheran. From Karaj, one heads toward Ghazvin, which is a town in the central province. Six kilometers from Karaj, one reaches the region of Sufiabad. In the distance can be seen a large building among a mass of trees. A first glance reveals it as a religious center. A crowd of people, young and old, can be seen dressed in long white gowns belted tightly around the waist, some with long hair, some with beards, and some carrying a two-headed axe called a *Tabarzin*. This axe is made of metal, usually steel, consisting of a long pole with two quite sharp blades shaped like moon crescents on the top.

The Oveyssi School: Karaj

Engraved on the blades and sometimes on the pole of the axes are the names "Tarigheh Oveyssi Shah Maghsoudi" and "Salaheddin Ali Nader." On the two crescents of the axes, the words "Ali Serrallah" (Ali, God's secret), Ali Vali al Allah (Ali, God's friend) respectively, are artistically engraved.

Some of the people seen outside are in fact guards of the Khaneghah, whose discipline and efficiency are the first thing to strike the newcomer. They greet one with a warm, polite and cheerful manner, and are quick to acquire permission for the newcomer to enter the Khaneghah. According to one's native language, one is introduced to a person or group with whom one may communicate.

The Khaneghah is entered through a small door, and once in the corridor, there are two ways to go. In one direction, through a small door, is the main hall, which is the gathering place for the men. The other way leads up some stairs to a balcony overlooking the main hall, which is the gathering place for the women. In the main hall, the master's seat, which is 77 centimeters high, is to be seen. The master steps in from one side, which is open. There is a doorstep made of black marble on which the master's right foot is engraved. Inside the area there is a large piece of buffalo skin stretched out on the floor. On a table, in front of a seat, lies a large Holy Koran, and in front on the ground lies a pale green marble stone which is protected with a glass cover. This is an empty tomb, which the master will eventually use, with a poem beautifully engraved on it; it is illuminated from within.

As customary, the walls of the hall are ornamented with various pictures of the Prophet and of the masters of this school. The artists, poets, writers, painters, moulders and engravers of these fine works are all followers of the school and have shown their devotion to it through their talents.

The main hall has three passageways to the outside yard. One is a small door near the Master's desk and is used only by him. Another door opens into a pantry and thereby to the kitchen, and the third door leads out to the museum, library, and the chapels.

The School's library has many treasures, the most notable of which is a collection of ancient handwritten books. (The holdings include approximately 12,000 scientific, literary and religious books). The students of the school spend their time studying and

The Masters Room

doing research in this library. At the time of the author's visit, a certain group was preparing a dictionary whose completion was imminent. It will serve as a reference in studying the work of any artist in the history of Iran. Another dictionary is in preparation which will provide an explanation of Sufi terminology in various languages, including English, which will aid translators. Due to the lack of translations of the cultural, scientific and literary works of Iran, much important material has never been available to the Western world. Therefore dictionaries seem to be the best first step for translators to take.

Next to the library are situated chapels for individual use. The ceilings of the chapels are beautifully moulded by craftsmen of Iran. Disciples who have achieved a certain state of holy consciousness are instructed by the Master to spend a period of time, usually forty days, in these chapels in order to pray and to purify their souls.

In addition to spiritual practices, according to his character, each person receives instructions in the certain physical practices from the Master. For example, the teacher might instruct one indi-

Library

Alchemy Room

vidual against excess eating, but might not give the same instructions to another. One of the principal doctrines of the school is to avoid doing anything in excess or in over-moderation. Nothing is to be done, however, without the teacher's command; for this reason, the spiritual teacher is most important.

Near the chapels is a laboratory where various experiments as well as spiritual instructions are carried out. Some of the work involves examination of the ancient science of alchemy or *Kymya* and *Exir*, another science related to alchemy. Kymya is the science of alchemy and Exir is an essence made through the science of alchemy. It has been said that Exir can change metals such as iron into pure gold. The word Kymya is sometimes used as Exir. Most scientists in the field of metallurgy will agree that there are innumerable untried experiments possible which combine various metals, using many possible catalysts and under different heating conditions. From master to disciple, over the centuries, many methods have been worked on and handed down. This body of knowledge is what the Sufis refer to as Alchemy.

The Professor and Master of this School has written about alchemy in his book of that title. He contends that a veil has been wrongly drawn over the secrets of this ancient science. Wishing to keep their knowledge from misuse, the ancient scientists did not explain it openly, and used codes to pass it on to people with a like mentality. As a consequence of this, the science has remained more or less incomprehensible. It is important that Western readers should not identify the science of "Kymya" with alchemy as practiced by early and medieval Europeans. The Persian subject opens a new world to the Western mind, and the "secrets" are by no means obscure or completely out of reach. However, as in any science of depth, there is much background which must be mastered and the subject itself must be studied very carefully.

A sauna and open bath stands next to the laboratory. This is inspired by the old Iranian aristocratic baths, but is constructed with a more delicate taste and is decorated with colorful ceramics engraved with writings. The floor is entirely made of marble.

In the center of this collection of buildings, a museum is under construction and is near completion. The museum has an octagonal shape, each side of which measures eleven meters inside and thirteen meters outside, the walls being 75 cm. thick. The heighth of the museum from ground level to the dome is 19.5 m, and from the basement level to the top of the dome is 25.5 m. Each of these numbers has a special significance, which in actuality constitutes an identification of this building. According to the science of letters of the Arabic alphabet, in which the Koran has been written, these numbers explain the sect and the set of beliefs of the group to which the building belongs.

In the entrance of the museum, one sees inscriptions on ceramic tiles in gold. Those represent the line of succession of the Oveyssi school and the genealogy of the Oveyssi Saints, and on other tiles appear lines written by Great Master Shah Maghsoud Sadegh Angha (the master of the school at the time of writing). The tiles have been executed by famous contemporary inscriptors. The plaster moulding in the chapels and in the museum is also worth noticing. It was likewise executed by followers of the Oveyssi School.

The weaving of Persian carpets is an unbelievably time-consuming craft. The entire process of collecting preparing and dying the wool or silk is done by skilled crafts-people without the use of machines. The first step in the manufacture of a woolen carpet is, of course, to shear the sheep. Then the wool is divided into strands by hand, sometimes with a light coating of beeswax on the fingers. The strands are then colored using natural dyes. The design is prepared and the frames for weaving are set up. Special combs for brushing the wool blades down are made by hand. Finally, the weaving begins, often with children helping—particularly in the knotting of the threads on the weaving stand and in the combing of each row of knots into position. It takes many years for the carpet to be completed and to reach the marketplace. It is a major activity in the lifetime of a family to produce just one carpet of any size or quality. In most Iranian villages, this art is practiced; women and children work and thus earn their living.

There are three carpets here which belong to the school. Two

Sculptor

contain the school's sign. This sign, which looks like a simple axe, is full of hidden and symbolic meanings.

As shown in the diagram, the upper part of the axe (or Tabarzin) is closely similar to the word "Allah" (God) and in the lower part of the ax the same word is written upside down as if seen through the horizontal axis as a mirror.

On one carpet, on the upper part of the carpet, there are some of the words of Shah Maghsoud Sadegh Angha about his father and Master:

"If our Master Mohammad, son of Abulfazl Angha, had not existed, the truth of cognition would never have been discovered in our time."

This carpet is beautifully executed in 64 shades of green. A third remarkable carpet is made of finely knotted silk in which the handwriting of Shah Maghsoud Sadegh Angha is woven in a circle—an endless saying, as it were. The tops of some of the letters reach symmetrically into the center of the circle.

These carpets are great works of art and have a great deal of symbolism. They are all the more remarkable when one realizes that they have been made by inexperienced people. The only exception is the carpet of the School's ensignia woven by the famous Iranian artist Rassam Arabzadeh (known as Arjang), who is also a devotee of this school.

The Master of the School

Professor Shah Maghsoud Sadegh Angha is the Master (Ghotb) of Oveyssi School and the great Master (Ghotb al-Aghtab) of Sufism in Iran. Shah Maghsoud, son of Mir Ghotb al-din Mohammad Angha,[2] was born February 4th, 1916 (Shaaban 15th, 1335 A.H.), in Teheran. He was a devotee of his father and after he later became a leader of the school.

Professor Angha has many works and the majority of his works have been translated into different languages.[3] He is one of the few people of this time who has the breadth of knowledge necessary to suggest changes in methods of thought, and to make certain aspects of religion understandable to science. The following are examples of his works:

"Enlighten the channel that extends from your heart to your brain and so not allow the heart and the brain to live apart, like two strange neighbors unaware of one another."

***

"When all the energies of your senses together reach your heart and lose the tendency to return, you will find yourself. And, when you are nourished from the source of life, heart, you will see your enlightened being."

***

"Polarize all your energies and concentrate them at this source of life in your heart until your findings become imperishable and your existence becomes stabilized, and then you will know eternity."

***

"Every bird flies back to its nest at nightfall, and there it comforts itself. And for you, gather all the strength that is spread out in your sense and body and concentrate them in your heart, and, manifest your luminous figure; if it inspires the eternal soul to the elements of your existence, you will step out of the realm of death."

Sessions of the School

The sessions of the Oveyssi School are held every Thursday night. The students (saleks), men and women, come from Teheran and other cities. The gathering starts at four p.m. and the saleks, after performing ablution (*Wuzu*), change their clothes for the session. (Wuzu is a kind of religious duty which every Moslem should perform before any prayer. They wash the exposed parts of their bodies. First, they wash their hands, up to the elbow, then they wash their faces, and then they wipe the top of their heads with a wet hand, and wash their feet up to the ankles.)

The outfit the saleks wear consists of a long white dress and pants and a long black belt. Some of the saleks have black robes to wear over their clothes. The robe has a golden band around the edge. The women have almost the same clothing, except that they wear skirts instead of pants, and white stockings. All saleks obey a strictly disciplined code of behavior during the session, since the sessions are holy.

After entering the holy place, each person sits in his or her own place. (If a person is absent, his/her place remains empty.) They sit on the carpeted floor on their knees. A special place is designated for newcomers who usually fall into two categories: those who come from other countries, like Egypt, India or western countries, and those who are the new students. The first ones are usually missionaries or researchers who want to know more about the School of Sufism; those who are students have been in other groups, and have been taught the introductory classes of the school by some of the experienced students and are now ready to come to the Khaneghah session. But being accepted in all the sessions of the classes does not necessarily mean that a given person has been accepted by the Great Master: the acceptance of the Master is only granted when the student is seen to be truly following God's leadership and has become a true worshipper.

At six o'clock, everyone maintains a quiet position waiting for the Master to come. They are all in a kind of meditation, so quiet that someone standing outside can hear nothing. The Great Master Shah Maghsoud Sadegh Angha enters the place through narrow door in front of the Khaneghah. He wears a cream-colored robe, with hand-sewn flowers around the edge. When he enters the Khaneghah, the strength of his presence produces an electrifying effect; he seats himself with great dignity at his special place.

His son, Salah-aldin Ali Nader, comes after him, wearing a white outfit like the other students with a long, black belt. However, his robe is purple velvet with a golden border, all hand-made. There is a special golden sign in the upper middle back of his robe. He sits at the left side of his father.

After seating himself, the Great Master takes a long look at the students and smiles at the newcomers in greeting. Then he begins to speak, and usually asks someone to read a verse of the Holy Koran, after which he comments on that verse. The sessions usually last for more than five hours. Afterwards, the Great Master permits the students to leave. They all stand, as they walk away, they do not once turn their backs to the place where the Master sits. They all leave slowly and quietly with their faces toward the place where he is seated.

There is another gathering held in the Khaneghah on the first Thursday of the lunar month (Islamic calendar). That night is called *niyaz*, the night for prayer. This gathering is like any other session except that at the end the Master permits the Circle of Zekr. The reader will recall that the Circle of Zekr consists of a group of students who sit in a circle to meditate and chant. This takes place in the middle of the Khaneghah with Salahaldin Ali Nader sitting at the starting point of the Circle. All participants hold a long rosary of beads. The light is turned off and a person starts the zekr by repeating a verse, "There is no other god besides Allah. "La-e-la-ha-ella-allah." Then all the students repeat the verse together.

This night is very significant for all students, whether experienced or uninitiated. It helps develop the understanding and the knowledge that there is nothing except God. He is everything and there is nothing but Him. After the zekr is finished, someone begins to pray and to beg God never to leave their hearts without the love of their Master, which leads to the love of God. After a few moments of stillness, the lights are turned on and the servers of the Khaneghah (who have the honor to "serve" others in the grand sense of Islamic tradition) start preparations for the dinner.

In addition to the ceremonies mentioned above, special sessions for various religious celebrations for New Year's day bring people from all over Iran to the Khaneghah. At the conclusion of such special ceremonies, the Great Master gives gold and silver coins to the people. These coins, which have the symbol and the history of the school engraved on them, are made each year.

Ceremonies Where the Cloak is Worn

The saleks all wear a white outfit on the evenings of the main sessions, along with a long black belt. They gain the privilege of wearing this clothing after having taken the classes and after having learned true meditation and inspiration; that is, when they have become true believers in Islam. When a Sufi reaches this stage and is ready to wear the cloak, a ceremony is held for him. The ceremony is customarily held during one of the religious celebrations.

The person to be granted the cloak must first wash himself all over, to remove any uncleanliness. There must be a concentration on the heart and a cleansing not only outside, but also inside. The initiate then enters the holy washing place which is built for this special ceremony. A group of initiated students then gathers around the initiate and recites some prayers. Then Salah-aldin Ali Nader, the son of the Great Master, baptizes the follower, sprinkles a few drops of water from a holy cup onto his head and shoulders, and writes the particular word, which has been given to this person to open up the heart, on his forehead. During this baptism, the follower is wearing an all-white towel. At the conclusion of the ceremony, everyone leaves the follower, who is then permitted to wear the overall white cloth. When ready, the salek comes out of the holy washing place, and in the company of the others, goes to the Khaneghah where the Great Master is in his place and the other students are seated to watch the ceremony.

The initiate, Salah-aldin Ali Nader, and the students who have accompanied the initiate stand in front of the Master's place, with their backs to the others and their faces to the Master. Then Salah-aldin Ali Nader fastens the belt around the salek's waist.

(The belt is a black bundle of forty black threads held together with forty knots, and is 110 cm. in length.) The Master then gives a cloak to Salah-aldin Nader, who passes it to the first person on his right. The cloak will then pass in turn from hand to hand and from left to right to the students who have accompanied the initiate from the beginning of the ceremony. After this the cloak is given back to Salah-aldin Nader. While this happens, the students all repeat a verse of the Koran or recite a prayer. Then Salah-aldin puts the cloak on the follower, who bows down to the Master, kisses the ground and returns to his seat. Others bring cakes and tea to the mass, and after a brief refreshment and celebration, the session resumes as the Master starts to teach.

Seyr Va Solook

It is difficult to describe this spiritual discipline. The main goal of a Sufi is cognition of "self" based on the words of the Prophet Mohammad: "Whoever knows himself truly knows his God." This state is understood to be the final and highest stage of any human being.

In the School of Tarighat Oveyssi, students are taught to put aside their desires, wishes and attachments to anything, and instead to love the eternal God. They are taught to pray and worship, so that God may open their ears, eyes and hearts to the realm of truth and to the light of the Holy Koran. They pray to God to lead them to the true path, which is the sole way of knowledge and cognition, and to introduce them to His teacher who will lead them to Him. The knowledge of that teacher is the knowledge of God. This teacher has lost his self-existence, and has come to the stage of rebirth, existing through God's existence—the stage of complete being.

In summary, it is through spiritual rebirth that Sufis gain their sight. Bodily death is seen as a desired goal; abandoning earthly life has already been foreshadowed by the Sufi's rejection of worldly values: death is a mere extension of this rejection; a movement toward the eternal. Each individual should strive as far as possible to mirror God's perfection. The ultimate goal of celestial re-birth is achieved by obeying the doctrine of true cognition, as taught by the masters, and through the guidance of God.

Appendix

Chapter 1

1 - Shah Maghsoud Sadegh Angha, *Chanteh* , 3rd Ed; Teheran 1965, p. 45.

2 - ALI, in Arabic alphabet (Abjad) contains three letters: "Ein," "Lam," "Ya," and according to the Abjad, "Ein" is 70, "Lam" is 30 and "Ya" is 10, which are equal to 110.

3 - Hajviri, Ghaznavi, *Kashf al-Mahjoob*, Teheran, Amir Kabir Publication, 1957.

4 - Attar, Sheikh Farid al-Din, *Tazkere al-Olia*, Teheran, Entesharat Markazi, 1964.

5 - Bagheri Namini, Sheikh Mohammad Ghader, *Aghtab Oveyssi*, Teheran, Amin Publication, 1973.

6 - The summary of the permission given by the great Master Hossein Dezfouli to Hazrat Mir Abulfazl Angha.

Chapter 2

1 - Abolghasem Ghoshairi, *Ghoshairi's Treatise*, Teheran, 1964.

2 - Abu Hamed Ghazali, *Ehyae Olom Din*, Cairo, 1939.

3 - Koran, Sura al Ansan, Verse 21.

4 - Shah Maghsoud Sadegh Angha, *Serr-al-Hajar* (Secrets of the stones), the book has been written in poetry. It is the most advanced in the series on Alchemy.

5 - A.Y. Arberry, *Islamic Culture*, India, 1936. pp. 369-389. Poem of Khayeh Abd-allah Ansari.

6 - Mah Talat Angha, from *Mohammad to Mohammad*, Teheran, 1977. p. 62. This book is translated to English.

7 - *Ibid.*, p.3.

8 - Jamal-al-din Mohammad Ghader Bagheri Namimi, *Aghtab Oveyssi*, Vol. 2, Teheran, 1977.

9 - *Ibid.*, p. 21.

10 - *Ibid.*, p. 148.

11 - *Ibid.*, p. 147.

12 - *Ibid.*, p.195.

13 - M.T. Angha, *From Mohammad to Mohammad.* p. 41.

14 - *Aghtab Oveyssi*, Vol. 3, p. 88.

15 - *Ibid.*, p. 252.

16 - *Ibid.*, p. 112.

17 - *From Mohammad to Mohammad*, p. 132.

18 - Shah Maghsoud Sadegh Angha, *al-Salat*, p. 12.

19 - *Ibid* ., p. 14.

20 - *Ibid.*, p. 9.

21 - *From Mohammad to Mohammad*, p. 193.

22 - *Aghtab Oveyssi*, Vol. 4, p. 202.

Chapter 3

1 - A poem of Jalal-al-din Ali Mir Abolfazl Angha, *Anvar gholob al-Salekin*, Teheran, Tahouri publisher, 1965, p. 23.

2 - *Ibid.*, p. 1. A poem: The aim of Sufism is not becoming a beggar;/ One can be a Sufi even while sitting on a throne.

3 - *Islam*, John Alden Williams, Ed., N.Y.: George Braziller, 1961. p. 140.

4 - *The Encyclopedia of Philosophy*, Paul Edwards, Ed. New York: Macmillan Publishing Company, Vol I, p. 416.

5 - Roozbeh: Son of Khushnodan known as Salman Farsi. He was an Iranian native from the state of Fars. At the first century of Hejrat, he became a muslim and one of the very true followers of Mohammad. He is one of the great Masters of a large group of Sufism, "Oveyssieh." He died at A.H. 37.

Chapter 4

1 - John Alden Williams, *Islam*, George Braziller, New York, 1961. p. 148.

2 - *Ibid.*, p. 149.

3 - *Nagel's Encyclopedia Guide, Iran*, Nagel publishers, Geneva, Paris, Munich, p. 310.

4 - *Aghtab Oveyssi*, Vol. II. p. 25.

5 - *Ibid.*, p.100.

6 - A.Y. Arbery, *Islamic Culture*, India, 1936. p. 350.

7 - *Ibid.*, pp. 369-389.

8 - The patriarch Abraham, ancestor of the Semites, is seen in the Koran as the prototype of the Muslim; it is implied that he arrived at monotheism by pure reason before the revelation came. With his first-born, Ismael, he built the temple of the Kaba at Mekka or Mecca, and instituted the rites of pilgrimage.

9 - Edward Fitzgerald, *Mantigr al-Tayr in Collected Works*, p. 196.

10 - Arthur J. Arbery, *Shiraz Persian City of Saint and Poets*.

Chapter 5

1 - The word "daravish" (poor) is a noun and adjective. Its similar word in Arabic is Fagris (Fakir). Daravish has come to be applied primarily to the adherent of a Sufi order. This word was mostly known in Kurdestan at the time of Abd-al-Ghader Gilani in the thirteenth century A.D., and then followed the Molavi order in Turkey, the Shadhili order of North Africa, and the Choshtiya of India.

2 - There are four accepted schools in Sunni Sect: Hanaffi, Maleki, Shafei, and Hanbali.

3 - Shah-Maghsoud Sedegh Angha, *Chanteh*, Behjat's publisher, Teheran, second edition, 1976, p. 54.

4 - *Ibid.*, p. 60.

5 - *Ibid.*, p. 72.

6 - Attar, *Tazkerat al-Olia*, Teheran, Markazi publisher, 1964, p. 42.

7 - *Ibid.*, p. 43.

8 - *Ibid.*, p. 52.

9 - Dr. Mohseni, Manouchehr, *'heikh Najm al-din Kobra*, Teheran, Iranian Books Publications, 1966, p. 64.

10 - Veys: a lover (in a famous Iranian love story).

11 - Ramin the beloved, of the same story.

12 - Bagheri, *Aghtab oveyssi*, Vol. I, Teheran, Amin publisher, 1974, pp. 133-346.

13 - *Ibid.*, p. 111.

14 - Jalal al-din Rumi as known as Molavi (died 1273 A.D.) son of Baha al-din Valad, a Persian poet and great Master of Sufism, whose father was a disciple of Sheikh Najm al-din Kobra Oveyssi. His family emigrated to Konya, the *saljugh*capital of Muslim Anatolia (Rum). He was also the follower and under the powerful influence of the Shams al-din Tabrizi, the disciples of Sheikh Najm al-din Kobra too. His great work is *Mathnavi*, a vast poem containing fables, theory and allegories on Sufism. He has another work in poetry called *Diwan Shams Tabriz*. Jalal-al-din is the founder of Mouilavi-ie, the "Whirling Daravishes."

15 - Jalal-al-din Ali Abulfazl Angha, *Anvar Gholob- al-Salekin*, Tahoori publisher, Teheran, 1965. p. 26.

16 - Shah Maghsoud Sadegh Angha, *Chanteh*, p. 226.

17 - *Koran* , Sura 68, Verse 1.

18 - *Chanteh*, p. 126.

Chapter 6

1 - Shah Maghsoud Sadegh Angha, *Ozan Va Mizan* (Weight and Balance). This is an advanced text on Alchemy. A major topic in Alchemy involves the transformation of metal from an imperfect

to a perfect state. The technology is very delicate and it is no wonder some people have believed that alchemy is an impossible fairy tale. Some scientists believed that if one could somehow combine chemical salts with precious metals, melting them together in a high heat, the existence of such a science as alchemy might be possible. An advanced science of this sort does exist. The key ingredient is termed *Hajar* (meaning "stone"). The great men who have inherited this science have talked or written of their experiments on secret codes referring to the ancient science of letters and numbers, which is a prerequisite for any investigator who wishes to read what has remained from the ancient practice of alchemy. The science of letters and numbers has been explained in *Kymya*, by Professor Shah Maghsoud.

2 - Mir Ghotb al-din Mohammad Angha, son of Jalal-al-din Ali Mir Abulfazl Angha. He was born in Teheran in 1894. He is the first master of this school who used the sciences to explain religious questions and made his followers learn and study sciences. He has many works, of which are: *Az Janin Ta Janan* (From Foetus to Heaven): A book analyzing the events of created man from foetus to the life after death. The book acquaints the reader with the realm of spirit and the life after physical death.

This book has been translated into Arabic and English. The English version is in press, and Arabic version has been published in Cairo, 1978.

3 - *The Mystery of Humanity* with an introduction by Dr. W.R. Brown, a professor of philosophy at Southwest Missouri State University in the United States; the English version was published in 1973 and German translation was published in 1978; Arabic version published in Cairo in 1975. (the book consists of three theses: Nirvan, Payame Del, Avaz Khodayan). Other works of Professor Angha which have been translated into other languages are:

Sahar, translated into English, published in America, 1981; published in Germany in 1978. The original language of the book is Japanese; *Sahar* was published in both the language of Farsi and Japanese in 1976.

Hidden Angels of Life, English version was published in America in 1976.

Al Rasael, Arabic version published in Cairo, 1978; Farsi version published in 1978.

Manifestations of Thought, English version published in America, 1980; Arabic translation published in Cairo, 1975.

The Traditional Medicine of Iran, a reply to Dr. Sidney Mitchell, English version is under printing in America (Farsi version was first published in 1976).

Professor Angha has more than 50 books (some published and some handwritten); all are kept in the library of Maktab Tarigh at Oveyssi Shah Maghsoudi in Karaj.

References

Angha, Jalal al-din Ali Mir Abulfazl. *Anvar al-Gholob al-Salekin; Haghayegh al-Managheb*. Teheran: Tahouri Publication, 1965

Angha, Mir Ghotb al-din Mohammed. *az Janin ta Janan*. Teheran: Tahouri Publication, 1963. (Translated into English and Arabic).

Angha, Mir Ghotb al-din Mohammad. *Tajalliat*. Teheran: Bank Meli Publication, 1963.

Angha, Shah Maghsoud Sadegh. *Chante*. Teheran: Tahouri Publication, 1965. (Translated into English.)

Angha, Shah Maghsoud Sadegh. *Mazamir Hagh va Golzar Omid*. Teheran: Zavar Publication, 1965.

Angha, Shah Maghsoud Sadegh. *Padid ehye Fekr*. Teheran: Tahouri Publication, 1966. (Translated into English as *Manifestation of Thought*, and published in America in 1980.)

Angha, Shah Maghsoud Sadegh. *The Mystery of Humanity*. Teheran: Amin Publication, 1973. (Fifth Edition.)

Angha, Shah Maghsoud Sadegh. *Hamaseh Hayat*. Teheran: Amin Publication, 1974. (Translated into English.)

Angha, Shah Maghsoud Sadegh. *Sahar*, Teheran: Oveyssi Publication, 1977. (Translated into English as *Dawn*. Published in America in (circa 1977); was also translated into German and published in Germany in 1978. (The original language of the book is Japanese.)

Angha, Shah Maghsoud. *The Hidden Angles of Life*. United States of America: Multidisciplinary Library Publication, 1975.

Arbery, A.J. *Sufism: An Account of the Mystics of Islam*. London: George Allen and Unwin Ltd, Publication, 1963.

Attar, Sheikh Farid al-Din. *Tazkere al-Olia*. Teheran: Entesharat Markazi, 1964.

Ansari, Khajeh Abd-Allah. *Tabegh at al-Sufi-ye*. Kabul: 1961.

Baghli Shirazi; Sheikh Roozbahan. *Abhar al-Asheghin.* Teheran: University publisher, 1969.

Bagheri Namini; Sheikh Mohammad Ghader. *Aghtab Oveyssi.* Teheran: Amin Publication, 1973.

Edwards, Paul, Ed. *The Encyclopedia of Philosophy.* New York: Macmillan Publishing Co., 1967.

Etemad Moghaddam Angha; Mah Talat. *az Mohammad ta Mohammad.* Teheran: Oveyssi School Publication, 1965.

Ghani, Ghasem. *The History of Sufism in Islam.* Teheran: Zavar Publication, 1954.

Hajviri, Ghaznavi. *Kashf al-Mahjoob.* Teheran: Amir Kabir Publication, 1957.

Hitti, Philip Khuri. *History of the Arabs.* New York: Macmillan & Co., 1951.

Junaid Shirazi; Moein al-din Abulghasem. *Shadal-Ozar.* Teheran: Abbas Eghbal Publication, 1949.

Junaid Shirazi; Moein al-din Abulghasem. *Hezar Mazar.* Shiraz: Ahmadi Jahan nama Publication, 1939.

Missignon, R. and Kraus, Eds. *Akhb ar al-Hallaj.* Paris: 1936.

Mahmoud, Ibn Osman. *Frerdos al-Morsheddi-ye.* Teheran: Zavar Publication, 1954.

Molavi Roumi, Jalal al-din Mohammad. *Masnavi Maanavi.* Teheran: Zavar Publication, 1936.

Mohseni, Manouchehr. *Sheikh Najm al-din Kobra.* Teheran: Iranian Books Publication, 1966.

Mehrin, Professor Abbas. *The Book of Sufism.* Teheran: Marefat Publication, 1954.

Negel. *Negel's Encyclopedia Guide.* Iran: Negal Publication, 1972.

Nicholson, R.A. *Studies in Islamic Mysticism.* Cambridge: 1941.

Nicholson, R.A. *Sufism.* London: 1959.

Persia I. Nagel Publication. Geneva: 1967.

Persia II. Negal Publishers. Geneva: 1967.

Rashad, Mohammad. *Sheikh Kabir Mohammad Ibn Khafif Shirazi.* Teheran: Andisheh Publication, 1971.

Rice, Cyprian, O.P. *The Persian Sufis.* London: George Allen and Union Ltd., 1964, Ruskin House Museum Street.

Trimingham, Y. Spencer. *The Sufi Orders in Islam*. Oxford University Press: 1971, London Oxford, New York.

Williams, John Aden, Ed. *Islam*. New York: George Braziller, 1951.

Yaaghobi, Ibn Vazeh. *al-Boldan*. Teheran: Bongah Tarjomeh va Nashr Ketab, 1957.

Glossary

Abol Ghasem Ghoshairi: The great Sufi who classified and defined many of the key concepts of behavior in Sufism in a clear and comprehensive book known as *Ghoshairi's Treatise*.

Abu Hamed Ghazali: A famous Iranian philosopher and Sufi who brought out a second major book on Sufi theory and terminology called *Ehyae Olom Din*.

After Hejrat: Designation of the Islamic calendar which marks the flight of Mohammad from Mecca to Medina after he had been warned of attempts on his life. The beginning of the Islamic calendar is thus termed 1 A.H. meaning *after the flight or migration*. This occurred in the year 612 A.D.

Ahl Hagh Darvish: These are the followers of Imam Ali.

Caliph: Among Islamics, a judge, governor or one in power in either civil or religious capacity.

Choshti-ieh: These are the followers of Khajeh Ahmad Abdel Choshti.

Circle of Zekr: This ceremony originated with the shattah Sufi Abu Saiid Abi al-Khair. His followers would sit around him in a circle and chant. It later developed into a special ceremony taking place in the Khaneghah. The master prays and then the followers begin to repeat a word, usually the name of Imam Ali, which is called the *zekr*.

Darvish: This is a synonymous word for Sufi. Unlike the Sufis who practiced the religion in Persia, however, the Darvish migrated to India. Both Sufis and Darvish are of the same religion having the same original lineage.

Ghaderi-ie: These are the followers of Sheikh Abu Mohammad Abd al-Ghader Gilani.

Housain Ibn Mansour Hallaj: The first man to be a martyr to his particular religious sect.

Imam Ali: Mohammad's cousin and son in law and first Master of the Shiite sect.

Khaneghah: Sufi place of worship, similar in appearance to a mosque.

Khergheh: The woolen cloak passed on from Mohammad to a succession of Sufi Masters.

Koran: The Holy Book of Islam. It uses ordinary words which also express an underlying metaphorical meaning that is not immediately obvious or accessible.

Maarofi-ie: These are the followers of Abu Mahfoz Maarof Karkhi. Their customs and genealogy are the same as the Neamatollahis.

Mecca: The holiest city of Islam. The Prophet Mohammad preached here for nine years.

Morshed: A master or instructor of Sufism.

Mt. Hira: The mountain to which the Prophet Mohammad made his retreat annually.

Naghsghband-die Darvish: These are the followers of Sheikh Baha al-Din Mohammad Bokharaie Naghshband.

Neamatollahi: These are the followers of Shah Neamatollah Vali.

Oveys Gharani: A follower of the Prophet Mohammad who succeeded his Robe.

Oveyssi-ie Darvish: These are the followers of Oveys Gharani.

Salek: An experienced man in Sufism.

Salman Farsi: One of the first eight followers of Mohammad.

Shiite sect: One of the two major sects in Islamic Sufism. The Shiites contend that Imam Ali assumed prominence as Islamic leader after the prophet Mohammad's death.

Sunni sect: One of the two major sects in Islamic Sufism. The Sunnis attribute equal significance to three religious leaders in addition to Imam Ali, who was proclaimed leader of the Islamic faith after the Prophet Mohammad's death.

Tasawof: To become a Sufi; it means *purity*.

Zahabiieh: These are the followers of Darvish Mohammad Mozahab Karandehi.

Index

Abd al-Ghader, 8
Adham, Ibraham, 50-51, 58, 59
Adham, Sultan Ebrahim, 30, 31, 48
Ablution, 21
Affection, 38
Agha, *see morshed*
Agreement, 36
Ahl Hagh Darvish, 71-72
Alchemy, 89-90
Ali, Imam, 6, 12, 18, 22, 63, 71, 76
Angha, Shah Maghsoud Sadegh, 90, 92, 92-93, 94-96, 96-97
Asam, Hatam, 59

Bagha, 19, 38
Baghdad, 8, 55
Baghdadi, Juanid, 55
Balkhi, Abu Ali Shaghigh, 59
Bironi, Abureyhan, 43-45
Buddha, Gautama, 50-51
Buddhism, 49-51

Caliph, 12
Certain Knowledge, 38
Chastity, 37
Christ, 63
Choshti-ieh, 78, 82
Choshti, Khajeh Ahmad, Abdal, 82
Christianity, 7, 17, 49, 75
Circle of Zekr, 22, 60, 64, 68, 95
Closeness, 39
Cognition, 32
Command, 38
Concentration in God, 34
Contemplation, 35

Darvish, 6, 67-68, 69, 71-72, 73, 80
Destination, 40
Devil, the, 29-30, 31
Devotion, 30, 35, 36
Dig Joosh, 22
Dispassionateness, 40
Dua, 31

Ebadat, 30, 35, 36
Ecstasy, 39
Ekhlas, 30, 37
Elm al-Yaghin, 38

Enabat, 34
Enbesat, 40
Endeavor, 35
Esgh va Jamal, 33
Eshagh, Sultan, 71
Exhilaration, 40

Faghr, 47
Familiarity, 39
Fana, 19, 37, 47, 60
Fard, 47
Farsi, 22, 43, 63
Farsi, Salman, 13, 51, 73, 75, 75-77
  see also genealogy chart, 77
Fear, 33, 37

Ghaderi-ie, 8, 68, 69
Gharani, Oveys, 13, 23, 32, 73-75, 76
Ghena, 19
Ghoshairi, Abol Ghasem, 27
  Ghoshairi's Treatise, 13, 27, 30
Ghorbat, 39
Ghotb, *see morshed*
Gilani, Sheikh Abu Mohammad Abd al-Ghader, 68-69
Gnosis, 38, 40
Goethe, 66
Gol Bang, 21

Hallaj, Housain Ibn Mansour, 55, 56, 57
Hejab, 30
Honesty, 37
Hope, 33
Houzoor, 39

Individuality, 40
Intuition, 39
Ivanov, 65

Judaism, 17

Karaj, 51, 72, 85
Karandehi, Darvish Mohammad Mozahab, 80
Karkhi, Abu Mahfoz Maarof, 81
Kashf, 39
Khaneghah, 12, 22, 51, 78, 80, 86, 94, 95, 96

Khergheh, 12, 23
Khivaghi, Sheikh Najm-aldin Kobra, 23-24
Khoaf, 37
Khurasan, 51, 58, 63
Khushu, 33
Koran, the, 13, 18, 19, 28, 31, 32, 49, 66, 87, 95, 97
Kurdestan, 8, 51, 67

Love and Beauty, 33

Maarofi-ieh, 78, 81
Marifa, 32
Marifat, 38
Mecca, 17, 18, 59
Medina, 18, 77
Mohammad, Prophet, 6, 12, 17, 18, 22, 31, 32, 33, 41, 44, 51, 73, 74, 75, 76, 87
Mohebbat, 38
Mojahedat, 35
Mokhalefat al nafs, 36
Molavi, Jalal al Din Mohammad Rumi, 79, 80
Moraghebat, 35
Morshed, 19, 37
Moslems, 18, 20
Mt. Hira, 17
Movafeghat, 36

Nader, Salah-aldin Ali, 94-95, 96-97
Naghshband-die Darvish, 69
Naghshband, Sheikh Baha-al Din Mohammad Bokharaie, 69
  see also genealogy chart, 79
Nahayat, 40
Neamatollahi, 22, 78
  see also genealogy chart, 79
Neyshapouri, Sheikh Farid aldin Attar, 60, 62
Nyat, 34

Obedience, 30, 36
Obstacles, 30
Ons, 39
Overcoming Passions, 36
Oveyssi school, 77, 83

Patience, 35
Permanence, 38
Pir, see morshed
Prayer, 31
Presence, 39

Raja, 33
Rememberance, 33, 35
Repentance, 35

Reza, 31, 36

Sabr, 35, 47
Safa, 45-46, 46
Salek, 12, 19, 20, 30
Satisfaction, 31, 36
Sedgh, 37, 47
Self-annihilation, 37, 60
Shiites, 6, 22, 58, 61, 63-64, 67, 71, 72, 81
Shiraz, 8, 63
Shirazi, Abu Abd-allah Khafif, 32
Shirazi, Abu Abd-allah Mohammad Khafif, 64
Shirazi, Khajeh Shams al-Din Mohammad Hafez, 66
Shirazi, Roozbahan Baghli, 32, 33
Shirazi, Sheikh Abu Mohammad Roozbahan Ibn Abi Naser Baghli, 64-65
Shouq, 39
Sophism, 43-45
Stage of being Overwhelmed, 40
Submission, 36
Sunnis, 6, 7, 67, 69

Tafrid, 40
Tahayor, 40
Tajrid, 40
Tarbazin, 85-86
Tarigheh, 24
Tark, 46
Tasawof, 12, 40, 46-47
Taslim, 36
Tavakkol, 31, 59
Tigh Bazi, 68
Touba, 35
Toubeh, 46
Tougha, 46
Touhid, 32
Trust in God, 31, 59
Truthfulness, 37

Unification, 32
Union, 39
Unity, 39

Vahdat, 39
Vali, Shah Neamatollah, 28, 78
Vara, 37
Velayat, 38
Vesal, 39

Wafa, 47
Willingness, 34

Zahabi-ieh, 78, 80-81
  see also genealogy chart, 8

www.ingramcontent.com/pod-product-compliance
Lightning Source LLC
LaVergne TN
LVHW021134080426
835509LV00010B/1349